WE ARE HERE

VILLAGE POETS ANTHOLOGY

WE ARE HERE

VILLAGE POETS ANTHOLOGY

Edited by

Maja Trochimczyk & Marlene Hitt

Moonrise Press, 2020

We Are Here: Village Poets Anthology
Edited by Maja Trochimczyk and Marlene Hitt

This book is published by Moonrise Press
P.O. Box 4288, Los Angeles – Sunland, CA 91041-4288,
www.moonrisepress.com; info@moonrisepress.com

© Copyright 2020 by Moonrise Press for this compilation only. All poems and essays by individual poets (c) Copyright by their authors.

Cover art © Copyright 2018 by Andrew Kolo, "Landscape with the Palm Tree" oil on canvas. Used by Permission. Cover design by Maja Trochimczyk. Font Book Antiqua for text, Times New Roman for biographical notes.

All Rights Reserved 2020 by Moonrise Press for this compilation only.

No part of this book may be reproduced or utilized in any form or by any means, electronic or mechanical, including photocopying and recording, or by any information storage and retrieval system, without permission in writing from the publisher and individual authors.

Manufactured in the United States of America

The Library of Congress Publication Data
Trochimczyk, Maja and Hitt, Marlene, editors
[Title] Village Poets Anthology (in English)
290 pages (xxvi pp. + 264 pp.) 15.2 cm x 22.9 cm.
Written in English. With introduction, portraits, and poets' biographical notes.

ISBN 978-1-945938-36-8 (e-book, e-Pub format)
ISBN 978-1-945938-39-9 (paperback)
ISBN 978-1-945938-40-5 (hardcover)

10 9 8 7 6 5 4 3 2 1

Preface

With this anthology of over 80 poets, we celebrate the tenth anniversary of Village Poets Monthly Readings, held since 2010 at Bolton Hall Museum in Tujunga. We also have occasional visits to the McGroarty Arts Center, a former home of the California Poet-Laureate in 1933-1944, John Steven McGroarty. His Poet-Laureate title inspired our local Poet-Laureate program, initiated in 1999, when one of us (Marlene Hitt) became the First Poet-Laureate of Sunland-Tujunga. The other editor (Maja Trochimczyk) was the Sixth and we just selected our Tenth, Alice Pero. A variety of public poetry readings, festivals and events followed, and the Village Poets Monthly Readings have been established as a result. You can read about the history of our readings further on.

Here, we would like to express our profound appreciation to all the poets who presented their work at the readings, both as featured and guest poets. We are also grateful to all the musicians and artists, who enriched our events with their talents, and to the entire Sunland-Tujunga community. Little Landers Historical Society allows us to use Bolton Hall Museum every month. The McGroarty Arts Center welcomes us every two years or so for our "Passing of the Laurels" ceremonies. Sunland-Tujunga Neighborhood Council offers financial support for some of our events.

We, the editors, are especially grateful to all volunteers who have made the Village Poets Monthly Readings possible: Lloyd Hitt, Bill Skiles, and other Poets-Laureate: Dorothy Skiles (the "president" and *spiritus movens* of our group), Joe DeCenzo, Elsa Samkow-Frausto, and Pamela Shea. Together, we have created something worthwhile, something lasting. Enjoy!

Maja Trochimczyk and Marlene Hitt

Table of Contents

Preface – vii
Table of Contents - viii
Poetry in the Foothills – A Look Back - x
Listing of Featured Poets and Artists – xii

Part 1. Featured and Guest Poets - 1

Lida Abramian - 3
    Be Me – 3
    Rite of Passage – 4
    Ancestor Love Dance – 4
Millicent Borges Accardi – 5
    Over Broken Bottles and Rivers – 5
    And Rage – A Pot of Orchids You Loved – 6
    Mourning Doves – 7
Sharon Alexander – 8
    Wheatfield with Crows – 8
    My Name Was Once an Argument - 9
Eliécer Almaguer – 10
    Acupuncturas – 10
    Acupunctures, transl. Margaret Saine – 11
Christopher Askew – 12
    There is a Place – 12
    Moments – 13
Beth Baird – 14
    This Table – 14
    Ode to a Temporary Relationship – 15
Judy Barrat – 16
    Remembering the Daisy Days – 16
Cile Borman – 18
    The Weekend – 18
    What is the Blues – 19
Madeleine Swift Butcher – 20
    What She Carries – 20
    Girl from Minneapolis – 21
Elena Karina Byrne – 22
    That Van Gogh Was on Drugs Wasn't Funny – 22

Don Kingfisher Campbell – 23
    Showing a DVD on the Galapagos to a Ninth Grade Class – 23
    Curiosity – 24

Ross Canton – 25
    "A Noiseless Spider" (Revisited) – 25
    Waking to Absence – 26

Gloriana Casey – 27
    The Magic of MOM – 27
    The Piggy Bank Blessing – 28

Jackie Chou – 29
    Ode to Insomniacs – 29
    Cerulean – 30

Teresa Mei Chuc – 31
    Pencil – 31

Jeanette Clough – 33
    Coloratura – 33
    Sky – 34

Beverly M. Collins – 35
    Dragon – 35
    Some Bridges – 36

Brendan Constantine – 37
    Anonymous – 37
    Difficult Listening Time – 38

Bill Cushing – 39
    Pelicans – 39
    Dispatches – 39
    A Former Life – 40

Marsha De La O – 41
    Summer – 41

Peggy Dobreer – 42
    Exquisite Harmonics – 42

Linda Dove – 44
    Fear Is the Key to Every Map, Every Eye - 44

Alexis Rhone Fancher – 45
    Overdose – 45
    Cruel Choices – 46

Mary Fitzpatrick – 47
    Basho's Death – 47
    Sweet Are the Uses of Adversity – 48

Michael C. Ford – 49
    A Get-Well Card – 49

Joyce Futa – 50
    Her Death – 50
    Kumquat Marmalade – 51
William Scott Galasso – 52
    Halcyon Days – 52
    May day manna (tanka) – 53
    Twenty-twenty (haiku) – 53
    One breath (haiku) – 53
Jerry Garcia – 54
    While Walking the Dog Last Evening – 54
John Guzlowski – 55
    Refugees – 55
    Thanksgiving Day Poem – 56
Charles Harmon – 57
    The Joy of Cooking – 57
Lloyd Hitt – 59
    A Shadow – 59
    Curiosity – 60
    Our Journey – 61
Lois P. Jones – 62
    Red Horse – 62
Georgia Jones-Davis – 63
    Monumental Dog – 63
    After the Storm – 64
C.E. Jordan – 65
    possum garden – 65
Mandy Kahn – 67
    The Tour Guide – 67
    The Everyday – 68
Mina Kirby – 69
    When I Was Me – 69
    A Special Place – 71
Andrew Kolo – 72
    America of An Immigrant – 72
    Dinosaur – 72
    Garden of Eden – 73
Deborah P Kolodji – 74
    white marble (haiku) – 74
    floating purple (haiku) – 74
    highway (haiku) – 74
    settling the estate (haiku) – 74
    the scarf (haiku) – 74

        morning tidepools (haiku) – 74
        winter sea (haiku) – 75
        a caterpillar's progress (haiku) – 75
        moon flower (haiku) – 75
        LA traffic (haiku) – 75
        our history (haiku) – 75
Mariko Kitakubo – 76
        Borderless Prayer (tanka sequence) – 76
Sharmagne Leland-St. John – 78
        Bruna Vieira gathers flowers – 78
        She Dreams – 79
James Levin – 80
        A.M. Ride – 80
Wayne Allen LeVine – 81
        No Way Back – 81
        Only This – 82
Stephen Lindsteadt – 83
        Saint-Rémy de Provence – 83
Elline Lipkin – 84
        My Parents Meet at La Grande Place – 84
        Limoncello – 85
B.D. Love – 86
        Declan IV – 86
Rick Lupert – 87
        Heat – 87
        Animal Hospitality – 88
Radomir Vojtech Luza – 89
        Tall Oak Trees with Gray, Flowing Moss – 89
Suzanne Lummis – 91
        Flour, Eggs, Milk, Baking Powder, Salt and God – 91
        Answer Like the House Burning Down – 93
        Not There – 95
Shahe Mankerian – 96
        Writer's Block at Father's Grocery Store – 96
Mirjana N. Radovanov Matarić – 97
        Land of Canyons and Arches – 97
        Oxymoron – 98
Maria Elena Mahler – 99
        La Machi – 99
Gabriel Meyer – 100
        A Harvest of Springs Struck by Lightning – 100
        Still Life, With Lilacs – 101

Naia – 102
    Songbird (haiku) – 102
    new love . . . (haiku) – 102
    in those moments (haiku) – 102
    the way his lips linger (haiku) – 102
    Ghosts Among the Cornflowers – 103

Toti O'Brien – 104
    Of the Palm – 104
    Albino – 105

Cece Peri – 106
    Trouble Down the Road –106
    Who Says Bodhisattvas Can't Have Fun? – 107

A.R. Peterson – 108
    Poem for Augustine – 108
    The Light That Fails – 109

Thelma T. Reyna – 110
    The Broken Heart Syndrome – 110
    This is How Grief Goes – 111

Cindy Rinne – 112
    Places I Belong When the World is Upside Down – 112
    The Land Owns Me – 113

Susan Rogers – 114
    Longing for October – 114
    Gratitude – 115

Sharon Rizk – 116
    Coming Up for Air – 116

Ed Rosenthal – 118
    The Digger – 118

Mary Kay Rummel – 120
    Burnt Dress – 120
    California Morning Song – 121

Sonya Sabanac – 122
    In that Banat Land – 122

Margaret Saine – 124
    Interlude 1900 – 124
    Awakening – 125

Shaymaa – 126
    Discover – 126
    Wild Life – 127

Param Sharma – 128
    Government Memorandum – 128

Rick Smith – 130
    St. Germaine District, Paris, 1949 – 130
Kathi Stafford – 131
    Near Belur Temple – 131
    Ripe Moon – 132
Julia Stein – 133
    After the Fire Storm – 133
Melissa Studdard – 134
    Inside the beige brick house, the beige rooms – 134
    My Kind – 135
Konrad Tademar Wilk – 136
    The Grace of a Great Dame – 136
    In Nonsymmetric, Entropic Gravitation – 137
Ambika Talwar – 138
    Quantum of Your Gaze – 138
    Love the Rain! – 139
Judith Terzi – 140
    Ode to Malala Yousafzai – 140
    Nostalgia – 141
Bory Thach – 142
    In the Moonlit Night – 142
    Lost Tribe – 143
G. Murray Thomas – 144
    "Your Kidney Just Arrived at Lax" – 144
Mary Torregrossa – 145
    The Promise of Snow – 145
Yun Wang – 147
    Futurescape – 147
    Spring – 148
Mari Werner – 149
    Joshua Trees – 149
    From the third planet orbiting the yellow dwarf star 27,000 light-years from the center of the 97-billionth galaxy – 150
    Measuring – 151
Kath Abela Wilson – 152
    Childhood Wisdom – 152
    Clear summer evening (tanka) – 152
    Like a painting (tanka) – 152
    Now a Garden – 153
    What grows – 154
Mariano Zaro – 155
    Synapse – 155

Part 2. Poets Laureate of Sunland-Tujunga - 157

John Steven McGroarty –159
    Biography – 159
    Just California – 160

Marlene Hitt – 161
    Biography – 161
    Arrival – 162
    Innocence – 163
    Enlightenment – 164
    Prescription – 164
    Ancestors – 165
    The Color of a Brisk and Leaping Day – 166
    Love Mended – 167
    The Remembering – 168

Katerina Canyon – 170
    Biography– 170
    Feet – 171
    Why Write? – 173
    The Color of Their Skin is What Defines Most People, so Barren – 175
    "O" – 175
    Material Value – 176
    Penance – 177
    A Cento for Poe – 178

Joe DeCenzo – 179
    Biography – 179
    Ordinary Rose – 180
    Conversing with Shadows – 181
    Barely Dressed – 183
    Flowers – 184
    My Companion in Free Fall – 186
    For a Friend–187

Damien Stednitz –188
    Biography – 188
    Sunland– 189
    This Smaller Murder – 191
    Details – 192

The Carter Variations – 193
To the Daughter I Didn't Have – 195

Ursula T. Gibson – 197
- Biography – 197
- The Summer Has Fled – 198
- Twelve – 199
- Driftwood Heart – 202
- Improvements – 201
- The Blossoms of the Night-Blooming Cereus – 202
- Time for Rest - 203

Maja Trochimczyk – 204
- Biography – 204
- What I Love in Sunland – 205
- Dragonfly Days – 206
- Sapphire – 208
- Arbor Cosmica – 209
- June in Gold and Blue – 210
- Imagine – A Poem of Light – 211

Dorothy Skiles – 212
- Biography – 212
- Taking the Old Road – 213
- Yesterday's Roses – 214
- Winds – 215
- Portland's Fog – 215
- The Scourge of 2020 – 216
- The Coyote's Howl – 217
- Deep in My Dreams – 218

Elsa Samkow-Frausto – 219
- Biography – 219
- Going – 220
- Late into the Night – 220
- Here, Alive & Awake – 221
- I No Longer Question I'm a Poet – 221
- Long Math (for Ander) – 222
- I Offer You a Moratorium on Race - 224

Pamela Shea – 225
> Biography – 225
> Glowing Girl – 226
> Eulogy for Night – 227
> Garden Visit – 228
> Lake Tahoe Vacations – 228
> Escondido – 229
> Rosebuds and Lovers – 230
> Supermoon – 231
> Wash Wonderland – 232

Alice Pero – 233
> Biography – 233
> Old Oak of Sunland/Tujunga Library – 234
> The Day of Nothing – 236
> Barter – 237
> Green by Water on St. Patrick's Day, Sunland – 238
> Rumors – 239

Biographies of Featured and Guest Poets – 239

Poetry in the Foothills – A Look Back

Village Poets of Sunland Tujunga is a group of former Poets Laureate of Sunland Tujunga who organize poetry readings in their community, write poetry, and publish books, making sure that poetry life is rich and vibrant in the foothills. Every two years or so Village Poets organize a competition for the Poet-Laureate of Sunland-Tujunga and, in order to involve the local community in the selection of its Poet-Laureate, establish a Poetry and Literature Committee of Sunland-Tujunga which selects the next Poet. After interviews and the decision of the committee to name the next Poet Laureate, a formal "Passing of the Laurels" Ceremony is held at the McGroarty Arts Center in Tujunga, in April, to coincide with the Poetry Month.

Another important project of Village Poets is the Monthly Village Poets Reading at Bolton Hall Museum in Tujunga, CA. Its tenth anniversary is celebrated in this anthology. You can read about past and future featured poets on the Village Poets Blog. The readings are announced in local papers, including The Voice of the Village and Crescenta Valley Weekly. This series was initiated in 2010 after Maja Trochimczyk was elected the Sixth Poet Laureate of Sunland Tujunga. Dorothy Skiles secured dates at Bolton Hall Museum – the fourth Sunday of each month (except December) at 4:30 pm – and the founding group has tirelessly worked together to make sure that the readings became a success. Dorothy Skiles books the dates with the Little Landers Historical Society that manages the Bolton Hall Museum. Marlene Hitt and Lloyd Hitt were in charge of the setup and the refreshments until 2019, when they retired from their roles and received a Lifetime Achievement Award for their selfless and generous contributions. Joe DeCenzo continues to make sure that chairs have their pillows, the mic was on, and poets stick to their allotted time. Maja Trochimczyk invites and schedules featured poets and artists; she also maintains Village Poets Website and the Village Poets Blog created in 2010 (villagepoets.blogspot.com).

During each successive Poet Laureate's term, the Poet joins the Village Poets planning committee – Elsa S. Frausto in 2014, Pamela Shea in 2017 and Alice Pero in 2020.

Eleven readings are held every year, so since April 2010 to March 2020, the Village Poets held 110 readings, featuring one or two poets each. Sometimes artists or musicians would appear alongside with the poets. Some poets returned more than once. A full list of events and poets is included below. The readings have been hosted by various members of the Village Poets Planning Committee – Joe DeCenzo, Dorothy Skiles, Maja Trochimczyk, Pamela Shea and Elsa S. Frausto. The events are held at Bolton Hall Museum, 10110 Commerce Avenue, Tujunga, CA 91042. They include a featured poet (25-30 min. for one poet, or 20 min. each for two poets) and two open mic segments. Refreshments are served and small cash donations collected for the cost of the venue. The museum celebrated its centennial in 2013; it is the second historical landmark in the City of Los Angeles.

The Village Poets Monthly Readings were instituted after two earlier poetry reading series were discontinued. The Eccentric Moon Poetry Readings and Camelback Readings were held at the Sunland-Tujunga Library, and chaired by Katerina Canyon and Elsa Samkow-Frausto respectively. Difficulty with securing space, appropriate hours that fit the poetry community as well as the library, and other considerations have caused the dissolution of each of these reading series.

The earlier predecessors for our 10-year series in the community was the Shouting Coyote Poetry Festival, organized by Katerina Canyon, the Second Poet Laureate. It was held on the front lawn of Verdugo High School and featured dozens of well-known Los Angeles poets. Joe DeCenzo later expanded Katerina Canyon's Shouting Coyote Poetry Festival into a huge Shouting Coyote Performing Arts Festival, held at Tierra del Sol in Shadow Hills. This Festival brought together many musicians and poets, performing on six stages in a grand celebration of poetry and music.

The Village Poets group also gives readings as a group, for instance, celebrating the National Poetry Month at the La Crescenta Library in April 2013, or during a special appearance at the Tujunga Library in April 2014. Other group presentations included several readings during art exhibits at the McGroarty Arts Center; a presentation at the Lit Crawl festival in North Hollywood in October 2016, and the Gathering of California Poets Laureate, hosted by Dana Gioia at the McGroarty Arts Center in October 2017. This event included workshops and well-attended public readings in which all 60 poets laureate from around the state participated.

Last but not least, every year, the Village Poets ride in the Fourth of July Parade of Sunland-Tujunga, in a beautifully decorated Poetry Convertible, giving away poetry bookmarks, postcards, or even fortune cookies – thus publicizing poetry in the local community.

The Poet Laureate Program

Sunland-Tujunga has had its share of poets and writers, with at least two poetry groups at any one time and a Poet Laureate program. The current Poet Laureate Program began as a tribute to John Steven and Ida McGroarty, who used their home as a gathering place for prominent town citizens to enjoy cultural and fundraising events. The McGroartys were probably the town's most famous citizens. John wrote a weekly column in the Los Angeles Times in which he romanticized the Beautiful Vale of Monte Vista and the town of Tujunga, full of wondrous attractions and good folks. A man of many talents, he was known as an orator, congressman, columnist, publisher, historian, playwright, poet and community activist.

McGroarty served as Poet Laureate of California, 1933-1944. The reading of one of his poems, "Just California", was required by all California elementary school students. Because of this legacy, Virginia Haddad, Tujunga poet and teacher at the McGroarty Arts

Center, decided that we should carry on the tradition in order to stress the importance of the artists and writers, past and present, of this community. She began, in 1999, a program to elect a person worthy enough to represent us as Poet Laureate. Many communities have caught on to this idea. At PoetsLaureate.com you can see photos of nearly all the California small town Poets Laureate. A Poet Laureate must be a writer who honors good craftsmanship and also be the most representative of the community.

For the two year term of our local Poet Laureate, he or she will have duties that challenge him or her to adapt well to a variety of occasions: the maker of a toast, the bestower of a prize, the dedication of a park, the composer of an ode to the Little League team and such. As well as a position of high honor, this is a position of community service. The poet Laureate is an ambassador, a cheer leader for our community. Many events have been hosted or enhanced by our poet ambassadors. All poets have written books. This program is part of the many faceted community activities in the 91040 and 91042 zip areas.

Marlene Hitt & Maja Trochimczyk

Alphabetic List of Poets, Artists and Musicians Featured at Village Poets Readings

Millicent Borges Accardi, 6/24/2011

Mark Achuff, classical guitar, 11/25/2018, with Westside Women Writers and the Krak Poetry Group (Kolo, Tademar Wilk, Trochimczyk)

Sharon Alexander, 6/28/2015, with Mary Torregrossa, 10/22/2017

Eliécer Almaguer, with Margaret Saine, 9/23/2018

Judy Barrat, 6/26/2016

Xochitl-Julisa Bermejo, 3/24/2013

Cile Borman, with Andrew Kolo, painter 11/24/2019

John Brantingham, The Sequoia Reading, 11/26/2017; with Michael C. Ford, 5/28/2017

Madeleine Swift Butcher, *Grateful Conversations* anthology, 11/25/2018

Jason Brain, 8/24/2013

Don Kingfisher Campbell, 4/22/2012

Ross Canton, with Teresa Mei Chuc, 1/25/2015

Gloria Casey, with Radomir Luza, 10/28/2018

Lisa Cheby, 1/22/2017

Monique Chmielewski Lehman, artist, with Judith Terzi, poet, 6/28/2017

Jackie Chou, with Joyce Futa, 1/26/2020

Teresa Mei Chuc, with Ross Canton, 1/25/2015; with Seven Dhar, 1/24/2016

Jeanette Clough, with Jack Cooper, 11/25/2015

Beverly M. Collins, 7/28/2013; *Mud in Magic*, 7/26/2015

Brendan Constantine, 3/22/2015

Jack Cooper, 8/24/2014, with J. Clough, 11/22/2015

Marsha de La O, with Jerry Garcia, 5/22/2016

Joe DeCenzo, in Village Poets Extravaganza, 3/25/2013 and *Meditations on Divine Names*, 7/22/2012

Bill Cushing, poetry, Chuck Corbisiero, guitar, *A Jazz Collaboration*, 7/24/2016; *The Lullaby of Teeth*, 3/25/2018

Seven Dhar, with Teresa Mei Chuc, 1/24/2016; with Abby Diamond, artist, 5/27/2018

Abby Diamond, artist, with Seven Dhar, 5/27/2018

Susan Dobay, with Ed Rosenthal, 11/24/2013, with Poets on Site, 1/28/2018

Peggy Dobreer and 100 Thousand Poets for Change - 9/28/2014; with Mandy Kahn, 3/24/2019

Heather Donavon and Steve McCormick, musicians, 8/28/2016

Linda Dove, 10/26/2014, with Judith Terzi, 9/22/2019

Alexis Rhone Fancher and Wayne Allen LeVine, 3/22/2020 rescheduled to 9/27/2020 due to COVID19

Sandy Fisher, artist; Pamela Shea, poet; 5/26/2019

Mary Fitzpatrick, 4/28/2019

Michael C. Ford, with John Brantingham, 5/28/2017

Alex M. Frankel, 6/23/2013

Elsa S. Frausto 1/27/2013, with Alice Pero in *Sunland Park Poems*, 3/26/2017; Passing of the Laurels, 4/23/2017

Joyce Futa, with Jackie Chou, 1/26/2020

William Scott Galasso, with Deborah P Kolodji, 2/25/2018

Eddy M. Gana Jr., with Stephanie Sajor, 2/28/2016

Jerry Garcia, with Marsha de la O, 5/22/2016

John Z. Guzlowski, 4/17/2011

Charles Harmon, with Mira Mataric, 7/22/2018

Sean Hill, with Apryl Skiles, 10/27/2013

Marlene Hitt, in Village Poets Extravaganza, 3/25/2013; *Meditations on Divine Names* Book Tour, 7/22/2012; with *Clocks and Water Drops*, and Brenda Petrakos, 5/24/2015; with Dorothy Skiles, 7/22/2017, Montrose Library; with Lloyd Hitt, Lifetime Achievement Award, 7/28/2019

Lois P. Jones, 11/25/2012; in Spiritual Quartet, with Ambika Talwar, Susan Rogers and Maja Trochimczyk), 3/27/2011; with Westside Women Writers, 8/23/2015; McGroarty Arts Center; with Alice Pero, 4/24/2016; *Night Ladder,* with Pam Shea, 8/27/2017

Georgia Jones-Davis, 8/28/2011, *Night School*, 3/20/2016

Christine Jordan, 6/24/2018

Mandy Kahn, with Douglas Kearney, 9/25/2016; with Peggy Dobreer, 3/24/2019

Douglas Kearney, with Mandy Kahn, 9/25/2016

Just Kibbe, 1/22/2012

Mina Kirby, 7/28/2013

Mariko Kitakubo with Kathabela Wilson, 3/23/2014; and with Bill Cushing, poetry, and Chuck Corbisiero, guitar, 7/24/2016

Deborah P Kolodji, 8/26/2012, with Naia, 11/27/2016; with William Scott Galasso, 2/25/2018

Andrzej Kolodziej (Andrew Kolo) with Krak Poetry Group, 11/25/2018; with Cile Borman 11/24/2019

Krak Poetry Group, 11/25/2018 (Andrew Kolo, Konrad Wilk, Maja Trochimczyk)

James Levin with J. Verl Silvester, 9/27/2015

Stephen Linsteadt, 10/28/2012, as painter in the *Woman in Metaphor* book, 1/26/2014

Elline Lipkin, Altadena Poet Laureate, 8/28/2016

Los Angeles Poet Society, 4/26/2015, at the McGroarty Arts Center

Suzanne Lummis, Honorary Member, California State Poetry Society, 10/27/2019

Rick Lupert, 11/20/2011

Radomir Luza, 2/26/2012; w. Gloria Casey, 10/28/2018

Maria Elena Mahler, *Woman in Metaphor* anthology inspired by Stephen Linsteadt, 1/26/2014

Shahe Mankerian with musicians Shandy & Eva, 10/23/2016

Mira Mataric with Charles Harmon, 7/22/2018

Neil McCarthy, 4/27/2013

Steve McCormick, with Heather Donavon, 8/28/2016

Meditations on Divine Names Book Tour with Maja Trochimczyk, 7/22/2012

Gabriel Meyer (with Elena Karina Byrne), 1/27/2019

Eric Morago, *The Lullaby of Teeth*, with Bill Cushing, Charles Webb, 3/25/2018

Naia, with Deborah P Kolodji, 11/27/2016

Ruth Nolan, 10/23/2011

Toti O'Brien , 2/24/2019

Passing of the Laurels Ceremony at McGroarty Arts Center, Dorothy Skiles, 4/15/2012, Elsa S. Frausto, 4/23/2014; Pam Shea, 4/23/2017

Alice Pero, 6/26/2011, with Lois P Jones, 4/24/2016; with Elsa Frausto, *Sunland Park Poems*, 3/26/2017; with Yun Wang, 8/25/2019

Andrew Peterson with Art Stucco and John Palmer, musicians, 4/22/2018

Brenda Petrakos, 5/24/2015

Thelma T. Reyna, with Beverly M. Collins, 7/26/2015

Cindy Rinne, 5/22/2011; with John Brantingham, in The Sequoia Reading, 11/26/2017; with Bory Thach, 5/24/2020, rescheduled to November 2020

Sharon Rizk, with Radomir Luza, 2/26/2012

Susan Rogers, with the Spiritual Quartet (with Lois P. Jones, Taoli-Ambika Talwar, and Maja Trochimczyk), 3/27/2011; with Westside Women Writers, McGroarty Arts Center, 8/23/2015; in *Grateful Conversations*, 11/25/2018

Luis J. Rodriguez, L.A. Poet Laureate, 10/25/2015

Ed Rosenthal, *The Desert Hat*, with Susan Dobay, 11/24/2013; new book, 6/28/2020

Mary Kay Rummel, 11/23/2014

Sonya Sabanac, 8/23/ 2015 with Westside Women Writers, McGroarty Arts Center; *Grateful Conversations,* with S. Rogers and M. Trochimczyk, 11/25/2018

Margaret Saine, *Lit Angels,* with Eva Zmijewska, guitar, 2/26/2017; *According to Nature,* with Eliécer Almaguer, 9/23/2018

Stephanie Sajor, with Eddy M. Gana Jr., 2/28/2016

Shaymaa, The Sequoia Reading, with John Brantingham and Cindy Rinne, 11/26/2017

Pamela Shea, Passing of the Laurels with Maja Trochimczyk 4/23/2017; with Lois P. Jones 8/27/2017

J. Verl Silvester, with James Levin, 9/27/2015

Apryl Skies, 10/27/2013

Dorothy Skiles, 9/25/2011, in *Meditations on Divine Names,* 7/22/2012, Passing of the Laurels, 4/15/2012, McGroarty Arts Center; 2/23/2014; with Marlene Hitt, 7/22/2017

Rick Smith, poet and musician, 2/23/2020

Shandy & Eva, musicians, with Shahe Mankerian, 10/23/2016

Sharmagne Leland St. John, 9/23/2012

Spiritual Quartet (Lois P. Jones, Taoli-Ambika Talwar, Susan Rogers and Maja Trochimczyk), 3/27/2011, and 8/23/2015

Kathi Stafford, 5/27/2012; with Westside Women Writers, 8/23/2015

Julia Stein, 6/22/2014

Art Stucco and John Palmer, musicians, with Andrew Peterson, 4/22/2018

Melissa Studdard, 6/23/2019

Ambika Talwar with the Spiritual Quartet (with Lois P. Jones, Susan Rogers and Maja Trochimczyk), 3/27/2011; My Greece, with Cece Peri, 9/24/2017

Judith Terzi, 5/26/2013; with Linda Dove, 9/22/2019

Bory Thach, with Cindy Rinne, 5/24/2020 rescheduled to 11/2020 due to COVID-19

G. Murray Thomas, 6/24/2012

Mary Torregrossa, with Sharon Alexander, 10/22/2017

Kathleen Travers, 1/23/2011

Maja Trochimczyk, Meditations on Divine Names, 7/22/2012; Passing of the Laurels to Dorothy Skiles, 4/15/2012; with the Spiritual Quartet, 3/27/2011; Westside Women Writers, 8/23/2015 at the McGroarty Arts Center; Slicing the Bread, 2/22/2015; with Krak Poetry Group, and Grateful Conversations, 1/25/2018

Village Poets Extravaganza, with Dorothy Skiles, Marlene Hitt, and Joe DeCenzo, 3/25/2012

Yun Wang, bilingual, with Alice Pero, flutist, 8/25/2019

Mari Werner, 2/27/2011

Westside Women Writers (Millicent Borges Accardi, Lois P. Jones, Susan Rogers, Maja Trochimczyk, and Sonya Sabanac) at the McGroarty Arts Center, 8/23/2015; with Susan Rogers, Sonya Sabanac, Maja Trochimczyk and Madeleine Butcher at Bolton Hall Museum, 11/25/2018

Konrad Tademar Wilk, Krak Poetry Group, 11/252018

Jessica Wilson, 8/24/2013; with Los Angeles Poet Society, 4/26/2015

Kathabela Wilson, with Mariko Kitakubo and Rick Wilson (flutes), 3/23/2014; The Art of Tanka. 8/26/2018

Mariano Zaro, 2/24/2013

Eva Zmijewska with Shandrelica - Eva and Shandy Duo, with Shahe Mankerian,10/23/2016; solo with poet Margaret Saine, 2/26/2017

PART 1

FEATURED AND GUEST POETS

LIDA ABRAMIAN

Be Me

I broke the vows ancestors had for me
Truth-seeking was transformation to be

I got confused, heartbreak came to me
Mind made stories, was obstacle for life

I unshackled, creative purpose for me
To gain clarity, to express inexpressible

I used a velvet hammer, not to break me
The beginning of "Work" for life ahead

I picked up a brush, invisibly painted me
Began sculpting with no clay in sight

I am an artist, I can express, I create me
Medium I used, be alive, be love, be me

Rite of Passage

The grand master said one day
Don't be disturbed by your joy
And if you distress by your fear
Both emotions certainly will
keep you in the depth of mind
But if you could tolerate both
Understanding joy, as you are
Seeing the fear, as fearless you are
Then, and only then, you will be
Certainly eligible, liberated to be free

Ancestor Love Dance

As I dance across the field
I see you weep, you murmur
It is my grave you stop to see
Beloved, I am not there, you see
Close your eyes, look with love
I am the breeze touching your face
I am earth, pebbles under your feet
And if you play in autumn rain
I will touch you, again and again
If you wake up by morning light
You will hear singing by river bank
Though my body, you may not see
But my being always will be
In your heart, if you let it be

MILLICENT BORGES ACCARDI

Over Broken Bottles and Rivers

We sailed, unequaled amid
a stupid sea of hard knocks.
You were no sharp match
for me, a somber artifact,
housebound for years, hidden
inside the world as I used to
know it would be. There were
once important times, when we
traveled, and then there
was wool. I touch your neck
like a weak signal, poor and too
ordinary to care anymore.
I am exactly what people think
of me, a dark mixture
of all I have lost. There is no one
to attract or bring home to me anymore.
The heavens, they are but a bright
whiff of distraction above, mere
remnants of the truth which is
just about to be voiced.

NOTE: First published in *Blue Collar Review* (2019)

And Rage – A Pot of Orchids You Loved

Three years the tense flowers
have bloomed from the
green shoots, dormant
for months, now, the nerve curling
around inside a glass bowl as if
it were a beginner. I am
reflective and filthy, in this
house, looking inside the gaps
in the floorboards
for substance, as if this is how
life is supposed to be, a clean
floor, newly painted walls
every few years, the kitchen
scrubbed within an inch of
its life, as my mother used to say.
Spiders long gone.
We are past the newly-minted
version of marriage, all choices of
avenues we used to have
have become deserted. There are
no strata to strike matches on.
With a nod and a fixed stare,
you tell me it will always
be this way, and I fear
many times that you are right.

(from a line by Inês Fonseca Santos)
Originally appeared in *Broadkill Review*, nominated for Pushcart

Mourning Doves

Have such soulful
Eyes, their gray suit
Of feathers blurs and sinks
Them into the background
Like a creature in hiding.
They hover below the wild
Bird feeder set up for the finches
And harvest the shells, the thistle
Seed casings and what drops after
The finches and faux robins and phoebes
Have feasted. The mourning
Doves huddle and nest in the mountains
Of seed shells and dirt and make circles
With their small bird bodies turning
Into the ground digging a place around
Them as if they were under a shrub with only
The black drops of ink from their tail feathers
Visible. In a group, they lie in wait, their dear gray
Eyes gloomy and sullen and innocent and they want
What the world desires, to be fed and comfortable
And consummated and happy.

SHARON ALEXANDER

Wheatfield with Crows

The night my father dies, I search for him
in the painting over his bed.
Crows clutter the sky,
wings rattle my windows —
the horizon crooked
as a broken bone.

Lost in the wheat fields, I find Van Gogh
painting the countryside yellow and blue, he sings
aloud to drown the ringing in his ears.

Blackbirds bow in silence,
clacking crows hold their tongues.
Van Gogh daubs the heavens
thick and thicker to obscure the uproar of red

poppies crowding him while the wheeling sky
shouts to be heard.
Somewhere my father hears dust storms
blow across the moon —
sunflowers choke the sky.

NOTE: First published in Alexander's
second chapbook, *Instructions In My Absence*.

My Name Was Once an Argument

I answer Yes to *Thunder Sky, Shrieking Hawk, Firefly.*

My name is the color of cactus bloom: tangerine, tiger stripe,
    marigold, marmalade, spice.

You can call me
    Lightning Strike, Tidal Wave, Raven's Eye.

My name was an argument my parents had.
    (I heard it from inside.)

Scarlett, my mother said. Then I heard nothing
    but her blood.

Over my dead body my father replied — the only argument
    he ever won.

Or you can call me
    Scarlet Fire, Hurricane, Riptide.

My name, the aroma of desert rain,
    soaks the Smoke Trees.

I slip my name beneath my pillow, hold its darkness
    under my tongue:
        Black-Eyed Honey Running Naked in a Field of White Horses.

NOTE: First published in Alexander's
second chapbook, *Instructions In My Absence*

ELIÉCER ALMAGUER

Acupunturas

Alguien dijo: existe un tejido central en tus versos, una idea obsesiva laborada febrilmente, con puntillismo, como esos artistas que hacen finas acupunturas en la piel del grabado. Me gustaría entender realmente cómo escribo. Cómo logro nombrar sin que me asfixien las palabras. Imagino que llegarán encapuchadas para sofocarme. Ella también quería oprimirse contra mí, como las envolturas donde los antiguos momificaban sus cadáveres. Estoy escribiendo un libro de poesía, quizás haga un silencio grande luego de su escritura, un silencio ancho y hermoso, en el cual no haya esta urgencia de renombrarlo todo. Deseo una soledad mía, no compartida ni con ella, que cuando suceda tenga el poder de anularme. Estoy escribiendo un libro extraño, no por original, todo lo rayaron en sus cavernas nuestros precursores. Lo auténtico es la entrega, que me desnudo siempre, que me desenvuelvo ante los ojos atónitos del auditorio.

Acupunctures

Somebody said: there exists a central fabric in your poetry, an obsessive idea feverishly elaborated, with pointillism, like those artists who do fine acupunctures on the skin of the engraving. I would really like to understand how I write. How I manage to name words, without them asphyxiating me. I imagine they might arrive hooded in order to suffocate me. She also wanted to weigh me down with herself, like the wraps with which the Ancients mummified their cadavers. I am writing a book of poetry, maybe I will create a big silence after having written it, a silence wide and beautiful, in which there would not be this urgency to rename everything. I want a solitude of my own, not shared with her at all, that when it happens it would have the power to annul me. I am writing a strange book, not because it is original, they have erased everything in their caves, our predecessors. The authentic thing is the engagement, I need to undress always, I need to put myself forth before the astonished eyes of the public.

Translated by Margaret Saine

CHRISTOPHER ASKEW

There Is a Place

there is a place
where sun and wind collide
with towering fortresses of rock and cloud
where time and rivers flowing
carve in ruddy plains deep spaces
vast and clear

in one such deep a hollow curves
a dimple in the palm of God

outside
the pageant of Creation plays
in billowing robes of rust and gold
on piercing fiercest blue
the fanfare of the bright and boisterous air

inside
there's calm
a flower grows

one day I'll take you there
and backs against the sheltering stone
faces to the flow
we'll listen 'til words wear away
and rest on silence
safe and whole.

Moments

Never mind that we crossed paths
among the avocado trees
Forget the bright wind tossing
auburn strands across your sagebrush eyes
Forget your sun-warmed hands
that held my arm as if I were a prize
to cherish, not a passing rambler
tumbling down the desert breeze.

Never mind we sat, your arm in mine,
beneath the orange-blossom skies
Forget we lingered as the sunset lined
your upturned face with gold
Forget how lilac shadows swept the hills
bade jasmine flowers unfold
to bathe us in their sweetness
as our small talk settled into sighs.

Never mind that we lay side by side
as seaside night turned bright and cold
Forget we fell into the well of stars
and, on the still-warm sand
soared through uncharted nebulae
in silence, 'til you found my hand
and pressed it to your heart
and pledged together we'd grow old.

Never mind our past
our precious moments shape us as we stand
but know however long the journey
you remain my promised land.

BETH BAIRD

This Table

Mom I have your table
Centering my life on it like you did
Visions of you late at night at this table
Your adding machine busy calculating
The bookkeeping for the family store
After dinner was cleared away
My brothers and I in bed
You put on your accounting hat
Do you see me on my computer late at night
paying bills on this table?

Hundreds of miles away and decades ago
So many people gathered at this table
To celebrate birthdays, graduations, holidays
With the traditional dessert passing of a See's Candy Box
Circulating the long oval table until it was finished
Relatives always photographed
Smiling around this table

Routine nightly dinners at this table
The TV blaring news from the Viet Nam War
Hard to stomach those meals when President Johnson
Started his message
"My Fellow Americans,
Tonight I come to you with a heavy heart."
Knots in my stomach with 3 brothers of draft age.

Do you see the people who enjoy this table now?
Do you see the tradition of long-stemmed candles lit for visitors?
Do you see me welcoming our relatives from across the pond to
this table?
I hope so   I see you at this table

Ode to a Temporary Relationship

Two years ago we met
A relationship not meant to last

I grew to depend on you
Constant companion
A font of knowledge
Answering my every question

Good times spent together
You entertained me with music, videos, games

You documented my existence
We took photos capturing moments
From our 753 days together

For this and more, I THANK YOU

But now you lie in state
I felt your energy slipping away
You could not hold your charge any longer

So regretfully I go
To ship away your remains
You left me no choice
I must replace you
With another phone

JUDY BARRAT

Remembering the Daisy Days

As children my best friend and I climbed a grassy hill
   that seemed to kiss the sky; it was dotted with flowers
We thought when we reached the top
   the clouds would be just within our reach.

Along the way we passed some trees,
   giant oaks and maples and a lone weeping willow.
And there were birds, bluebirds and robins
   and we thought "this is where they learn to sing".

Once at the top we'd sit in the cool grass
   picking honeysuckle, drinking nectar from the stems.
We held buttercups to each other's chins
   to see the bright yellow reflection on our faces.

And then there were of course, the wild daisies
   which swayed in the grass and called for us
to pick one to determine whether the boys we liked
   liked us back – he loves me, he loves me not.

Now all grown up I wander through a field
   of flowers and stoop down to pick a daisy.
I gaze at this lovely perfect flower which seems to
   look right back at me with its big yellow eye.

Reminded as I am, of those carefree daisy days,
   I look around, find myself alone and begin
One by one to gently pull petals until
   the last petal is gone: "he loves me not".

He loves me not? – I stare in disbelief at
   that unblinking yellow eye
and with childlike petulance, tearfully cry:
   "Is that your final answer?"

CILE BORMAN

The Weekend

Telephone poles marching,
Tumble weed rolling,
I miss your touch, so very much,
The radio keeps me company,
The songs while the miles away,
I realize you never think of me anymore,
And it hurts, because I still think of you,
I pause at a crossroad to brush away a tear,
I wish you were near, sitting right here,
Sharing the landmarks that we use to share,
I remind myself again, that you no longer care,
Golden aspen beside a stream,
I pause to take in the view and to dream,
Ahead in the distance, the desert is aglow,
With the lights of the city, that we used to know,
I check in downtown,
 and walk the blazing streets where we use to go,
I miss you so,
From my window I view,
a neon cowboy waving at me, he reminds me of you
I decide to take in a show, I'll dine alone,

At a place where we use to go,
I still miss you so,
I watch the couples and at first I feel jealousy,
My eyes fill with tears, because now I see,
I needed this weekend to revisit the past,
So I dress for the road,
I change my perfume,
I'm on the move again, and not a moment too soon
Headed back to the city the future is clear,
The journey to the past, was bitter-sweet,
A place where ghosts live and meet,
Love never dies, it only changes.

What is the Blues

What is the blues
How do you feel it
When do you know when
You got the blues
Who is the blues man
How is he feelin'
What makes him able
To sing the blues

There was Buddy Bolden
Out of the delta
And Louie Armstrong
Out of the waif's home
Bessie Smith & Big Momma Thornton
Singin their hearts out
While livin' the blues

How do you feel it
Where do you find it

What is the blues
How do you know
How is it written
Where is the rhythm
What are the chords
To make it so

Displaced manhood
Corrupted womanhood
Too many children
Up to no good
Blood on the highway
Blood in the tall trees
People gone mad, crying the blues

The blues is a lifestyle
Painful and half wild
Stabbing your insides
Sucking your bones dry
The blues is a feelin'
That keeps you reelin
Searchin' for something
To ease the pain

I hear the outcry, the lyrics don't lie
They make my blood run, hot & cold
I hear the wailing I know the torment
I feel the pain, down deep in my soul

…………...that is the blues

MADELEINE SWIFT BUTCHER

What She Carries

She carries her mother on her back,
her corrections and manners, 'return hate
with love', she folds in compassion -
'Think of how someone must feel
to behave like that.'

She carried grief and shame,
shame and guilt for not being the One
her mother thought her to be
she carried on as to not carry on
would be a mortal blow.

She mourned her younger quick self
so full of her whole happiness.

She carried a full weight that was never
hers, of others, and it made the going
harder and made her stronger in the
wrong places to feel like a beast hiding
in the shadows of the woods barely
able to walk.

Girl from Minneapolis
May 30, 2020

The rock is massive and still -
a black granite overhang struck
through with quartz, zig zagging
lines of a lost language,
her own hidden shelter from childhood -

she sits under it a long time
in the silence of no thoughts,
her refuge - removed

from a world swirling
in pain, spinning, unraveling,

she holds her knees to her
chest and rocks rhythmically,

calling for
a way to think,
a way to understand,
a way to intuit -

drowning in this historic loss
so new to her,
rocking and rocking,
how could she have not known?

She pulls her blue t-shirt around her
and strides out into the driving rain
quickly soaked through, she walks
through the dark woods she's known
all her life -

her penance -
her strength -
grow with every step.

ELENA KARINA BYRNE

That Van Gogh Was on Drugs Wasn't Funny

the comedian said, which is why his sunflowers' yellows
were so very yellow in their deliberately askew heads, and
from there now I know too, bees can dream, which must be
a kind of drunken wavering from the sun, dizzy parallax of
dance to dance flower-color crowned in the mouth's epiphany
carried home. Hive's hexagon. Sunflower's Fibonacci. Love is
this precise, yet so lie-lawless once let loose inside the body, all
Nile and noontime, black seed and spiral, to a hint of foreground-
yellow paint between the teeth. I desire something new every day,
like his later alterations, wet from another's hands placed so very
carefully over me with the unleashed look of light. That is where
we know *nothing but sunflowers*, we become a different version.

NOTE: This poem will appear in Byrne's October 2021 Omnidawn
ekphrastic poetry book, *If This Makes You Nervous*.

DON KINGFISHER CAMPBELL

Showing a DVD on the Galapagos to a Ninth Grade Class

Some watch the projected video
of blue footed boobies
diving down like bombers
to feast on an unsuspecting school of fish

Others would rather stare
into small lighted rectangles
to play a game, send messages
or simply check out their faces

The British narratress
twistedly intones the wonder
of sea lions snatching by the tail
swimming rock-colored iguanas

And what will become
of the fourteen-year-olds
who don't want to take notes
on this predatory world

The gliding hawk seizes
the frantically running lizard
The bug-eyed orange crabs
pinch off pieces of wounded seagull

Are these students doomed
to be pushing paper, repairing roads
selling cars, hammering homes
stocking stores, serving plates

The volcanic islands themselves
are born in the ocean
live a few million years
sink slowly to die

Curiosity

Why can't I walk
On this pebbly dirt

Why can't I traipse
Up rocky brown slopes

Why can't I climb
Ridge by ridge plateau

Just because it is too far
To reach without a ship

Just because there's not
Enough money for a mission

Just because I will be dead
Before an expedition leaves

At least I can enjoy the robot
Photographs from the rover

And without hesitation believe
I am seeing familiar earth

Minus plants, animals... now
Sporting human-made debris

ROSS CANTON

"A Noiseless Spider" (Revisited)
(for Walt)

Just a fuzzed blur of legs fleeing across the rim
of my eyes—but then the tiny, black body leaps off
and hangs mid-air, ten inches or so below my lenses—

too far from the ground to jump, nothing near enough
to send a line to unless I tip my head so he can repel
onto my chest and skitter across the elephant grass

sprouting from my Hawaiian shirt—and so he simply
dangles there, swinging and twisting like a window-
washer fallen from the scaffolding of a tall, tall

building, dangles--upside down, legs working hard
to secure a hold—no before nor after, no god to know
the gossamer's meaning as he spews out another

thread to hold him, nothing but my hand pulling
the filament off my glasses and holding him between
two fingers, holding, then raising him up so I can

finally fix him in my sight as he swings back and
forth as if on a pendulum, holding, and then, care-
fully, carrying him outside where a slight breeze

catches and throws him above my head as I open the
door, throws and almost sets him free--till I lay him
down on a blade of grass where he lies still, feigning
death, before suddenly scuttling away, vanishing into
a crevice of dark, green, bodiless shadow--O my soul!

Waking to Absence

Nothing new, just another black
molly among black mollies
gone — each unnamed, common,
no red stripe nor gold splotch
to distinguish the gone one
from the three still doing laps
round the coral trees, and yet,
having awakened so — sun
still swimming in the shadows
beneath the hills, my mother
sleeping in a home somewhere,
her flesh no longer communing
with her mind — having awakened
to this space left when a body
is swallowed after death, I press
my finger against the glass and
mark the place where loss remains.
Years, a year, a day, this wakeful
moment, this pink rose sky
blossoming from nightshade as it
crowns from the ridgeline — her face
bloomed to ashes, his to bone, mine
to this O, O, and out there, there
where the horizon ends and our
image-laden world begins, so my
morning begins, in darkness
fading, in what is not, but out of
that absence I sow the stars, the
verdant grass, the fish in their
tank of simple knowing, out of
that longing I sing what's left
of song

GLORIANA CASEY

The Magic of MOM

Oh, MOM, your name's a palindrome;
it's letters they form that.
It reads MOM going to the right.
From left? It reads MOM back!

Dependable that MOM word is,
in quality so true.
The YOU we always do count on,
Today, you get your due!

Three hundred sixty-five the days,
just one we celebrate.
We ought to celebrate you more;
perhaps a weekly fete?

A magic MOM in ambigram,
so please, do take a bow!
For even more— —just flip that name,
and MOM turns into WOW!

NOTE: originally appeared in altadenablog 2012

The Piggy Bank Blessing

The HE yells," Charge, but SHE yells, "save!"
Dilemma! Oh so common!
A frugal SHE, yet spendthrift HE.
Finances had hit bottom!

They tried the ice cube frozen test,
where card must thaw to spend.
"Oh my," the weary wife did say,
"HIS patience has no end!"

Then next they tried to list all down,
Each purchase to the cent.
But found the pen and paper bills,
In costs , made not a dent.

"Ah ha," HE said. "I have a thought—
it does seem a bit wiggy.
Each time I charge---- the interest costs,
We'll put in our bank, Piggy."

With calculator in his hand,
charge card was wrapped in tape.
He had to figure interest first,
Soon patience met with fate.

"I'm spending that!" He winced in pain.
"This interest costs us dearly."
SHE saw his transformation there,
A man was saved, quite clearly.

So HE and SHE, they danced through life,
Both were a little giddy.
Their "interest," game had saved their lives.
They owed it all to, "Piggy!"

JACKIE CHOU

Ode to Insomniacs

When you're up with the owls and moon people,
I'm in a cozy slumber, deep in dreams.

You can do so much;
String together stars,
Enough to feed a whole village
Come morning.

Your eyelids droop with weariness.
You remind me of mama and papa

Who worked till their bones broke,
While I lay indolent, on a couch,
Embarrassed by their smelly armpits

Urged them to eat well, sleep well,
And bathe daily. To no avail, my voice
was smaller than their American dream.

They both died young,
And you and your sleepless nights,
Traumatize me all over again.

Cerulean

My mother clad me in pink,
and later in my teens, lavender.
But the blue was always there,
underneath the pastel colors.
It was in my genes,
blue with its melancholia
and myriad synonyms,
azure and cerulean.
My mood is a spectrum
of different shades of blue,
including royal and navy.
The sky and the sea are blue,
with every variation in between,
turquoise and indigo.
Blue is behind my strawberry colored smile.

TERESA MEI CHUC

Pencil

> *"In spite of everything I shall rise again: I will take up my pencil, which I have forsaken in my great discouragement, and I will go on with my drawing."* - Vincent Van Gogh

A missile is shaped like a pencil -
its long, slender body and pointed
end creates history.

A girl walking down the street
a few steps ahead of her sister and friend,
two medics who were trying to help
injured people, the parked ambulance -
all were annihilated by the same weapon.

Above, drones - silent, unmanned planes.
A metal, predatory bird that shoots a missile
with precision, identifying the colors of a shirt,

the features on a face - the shape of a nose,

the color and length of a mustache.

In a room far away, in another country, a man
sits at a desk and looks at a screen; he strokes
his thick, dark mustache as he carefully
contemplates, then pushes a button.

There is a charred hole in the ground
where the girl once stood.

There are pencils that write and erase,
write and erase, so that there is nothing
to be read on the page. The page blank
as the desert sky, blank as the smooth shell of a drone.

There is a family drinking mint tea
in a living room.
The man holds a cup to his lips,
the glass touches his mustache.

A silent bird hovers above.
In a split second, everyone is dead,
the house is in rubbles - arms, legs,
splattered organs among broken concrete.

Soon, there will be no trace.

NOTE: *Pencil* first appeared in *Mo Chapbook* (Silkworms Ink)
and *The Good Men Project* http://goodmenproject.com/
featured-content/chb-pencil/

JEANETTE CLOUGH

Coloratura

The woman next to me in the concert hall does not remember anything for long. She can inhabit only a moment. It doesn't matter. Music is the same way. Her daughter fills in mama's blanks. *Is this your new house?* mama asks. *No,* says the daughter, *we come here to listen to music.* When the coloratura walks onstage in a flowing white gown with sparkly heart-shaped bodice and singing high notes the mother gasps, and gasps again two or three times when the soprano ascends yet another octave. The daughter seldom sees her so entranced and takes her mother's picture with the cell phone, making a flash during the concert. During intermission she apologizes. *I am mortified,* the daughter says. *We hardly ever see her this way.* Mama spreads her hands and says, *Unmortify, unmortify. It is beautiful.*

NOTE: Published in *Angle of Reflection*, Arctos Press, 2017.

Sky

Sky starts at ground level. Whatever level the ground is,
sky starts there.

Sky travels. It cannot *not* travel.

Notice how sky almost repeats itself with small variations
of cloud; with shades of blue and gray.

Tomorrow, sky may bring rain.

The color of sky is subjunctive. It speaks in run-on sentences.
Other times in fragments.

Some days, sky is all margin. It wraps around everything.
There is nothing it will not swaddle.

When you breathe in, sky breathes out.

Sky fills the space between. Just now, it came through
a closed window.

Sometimes sky scrims the sun like a geisha's fan, a peacock,
a royal flush.

A stone will store pieces of sky. Sky does this when it wants
to rest. If you lose jewelry, that's sky getting free.

Sky will store pieces of stone. Stone does this when it wants
to move quickly. If you live on a planet, that's stone getting free.

When sky listens, it makes the sound of a caterpillar spinning.

A caterpillar spinning makes the same sound as sky.

                      NOTE: Published in *Flourish*, Tebot Bach Press, 2017.

BEVERLY M. COLLINS

Dragon

With eyes like emeralds…Its
voice blows fire until lives change shape.
Many are like clouds drug by the claws of the
wind, in new directions. Notice when a
pillow-like surface bears the tell-tale
pitter patter that something more lurks ready
to plant itself sweet as carbon monoxide's kiss.

A quiver felt by one of the 5 senses while
completely undetected by the others.
It exists as a pre-warning and an aftermath
In the same casing. Pregnant with storm
Yet calm in appearance.

How many of us remember being part
of thunder's story as it grew lightening?
Each new day-dreaded as gun powder's scream.
Living through moments that cause one to feel
as muted as an unfinished thesis in a side cabinet.

The Dragon invites all to warm up
near the fires that will sting some into ashes.
Its promise presents a haven that is;
the "I" in team just out of view,
soft lips on a chicken and a bear that never
craps in a wooded area-believable.

Yet, pressure is one factor that grow muscle.
And, life is empty without the thrill of a
possibility to step upon the rocks that could burn.
So, we soldier on.

Some Bridges

Grimace in silence against the weight
that presses them. Like the quiet look
from one's father. An inaudible support
sure, in its reach and sometimes,

a comforting presence that's taken for
granted like the shelter enjoyed by an
umbrella-most quickly put aside once we
have entered the doorway of a house.

Some bridges offer passage while they are
themselves; unhinged. They give a feeling of
safety as long as one does not look closely.

For it is fear itself that is the undoing of a climber
Those who fall, first imagine the slip of their feet
from a step-of-certainty.

On boat rides, I love to view the underside of
bridges. Their skeleton exposed…It reveals the history
of cries and a closet-of-cracks that stare back at the
viewer and dare anyone to speak a word of their existence.

BRENDAN CONSTANTINE

Anonymous

this desk that traveled by ship
and the lamp that still belongs
to a dead man
the folded paper horse that falls
from my favorite book

the picture on its cover
of a girl holding a parrot
one an afternoon in 1640

the 17th century still
somewhere under this house
the hardest surprise is
there isn't one

the box of bottles outside
my neighbor's door
how they shudder
when he comes home

the lost button on my shirt
like a tiny skull
you'd find inside an aspirin
and this expensive keyboard
the ring of grime around
the one marked 'return'

Difficult Listening Time

A flock of pink flamingos moved in
across the street, and set up plastic people
on the lawn.
                They've faced them out
this way, hands molded to their chins,
looking more like us as night comes on.

Downtown, the waitresses are starving
in their aprons; the watchmen get fainter
by the hour.
                It's Difficult Listening Time,
object response time, time for 'the tears
of things.'
                There has to be a way to help
it along, a way to dry the rain as it falls
so we can keep these clothes.
                Let's go
to the woods & hang a painting of this
room on every tree. We'll go to sea
& on each sailboat fix a picture
of a hotel bed.
                Or how about we stay
home & talk out every song between us
until we sound like heavy, stupid birds.

NOTE: This poem first appeared in the journal *Ploughshares*. It can currently be found in the collection *'Calamity Joe'* (2012 Red Hen Press)

BILL CUSHING

Pelicans

Slowly circling,
the pelican

drops like a stone
into water.

Then climbing the
air, he stops, and

with a single
motion of wings,

glides on the wind.

Dispatches

In the end, if she
was not oblivious, my
mother's saboteur
steeped her in dementia
making death more like a cure.

Dad hugged me at ten
when his mother died; then years,
my ire, and our pride
split us so that his passing
deterred us from another.

A Former Life

I thought I saw John Fox today
riding the red Schwinn
it seemed he always had.
Then looking right, I saw a dog
that might have been Heidi
except it was a lab.

And stopping
for those seconds
on that street,
I waited
to smell
honeysuckle, but

the bike was quiet, lacking
clothes-pinned baseball cards
clattering against spokes;
then the ground the dog played on
returned to today, and
instantly, so did I.

MARSHA DE LA O

Summer

as far south as possible – to live – the ache
on the edge of what can't be endured,
Monterey cypress on the spit, this remnant –
when will longing be done with me –
parched, parched St. Catherine's Lace
fuming her last, and Sister Datura,
mi loca, my girl, her closed mouth
twisted like paper, horses in the
shallows, piebald and panicked, rearing
in the foam, ghost eyes wide, oh
far-ranging roans, blue multitudes
why oh why can't I, rushing the horizon –
naturally I dream the length of summer
days & nights when the moon lives
for weeks in my room, staggering in late
every night drunk, slip sliding off her
shoulders into an ivory pool on the carpet
and still she will not ease me

PEGGY DOBREER

Exquisite Harmonics

What is exquisite
      is the breaking of china
           splash against tile
      bright tones of glass

What is exquisite
      is the tango of Kali
           The savory statement
of unsung stanzas
The brain quenching
      fire of mouths

Migration of the herd
      to the gate of the mind
           Throne of the flesh
                  that lights up the eye
                       Arc of the rib to
                            the bone in the soup

What is exquisite
      is a memoir of the body
           A vibratory tonic of
connective harmonics
guiding chants that
                cannot be extinguished

What is exquisite
      is this limitless unleadening
           alchemy of Ganesh on our sleeves

In the breath
      of the opening cage
            the rush to rhapsody's rest
                  in the eyes of the hawk
                        on the wings of a loon
                              who light this way and
                                      fill these forests with
sound

NOTE: first published in *Drop & Dazzle*, MoonTide Press, 2018.

LINDA DOVE

Fear Is the Key to Every Map, Every Eye

It always starts with fear. Isn't that what is
at the bottom of every well, which is a story

told with water but is really about the rope-
puller or the face in the skim of the bucket.

The body always begins with a short object.
A gun or a bird. Perhaps an idea. It

is always changing its shape, covering
for spilled sins like a Persian carpet

with a thick pile of pink and blue fur. It
substitutes one thing for another, one fear

for a coin, one fear for a fern, one for an
unburned house. You can't see the eye

of the polar bear from where you're standing
because it looks like a stone in the snow. It

is safer to look at fear in a box, to pull fox-
gloves over your hands like suits of petals.

NOTE: published in *Fearn*, Cooper Dillon Books, 2019.

ALEXIS RHONE FANCHER

Overdose

No, he did not look natural in his coffin.
He is not in a better place.

Don't compare your pain to mine. Your dog
getting hit by a truck is not the same.

You really don't know how I feel.

Don't say you're devastated.
Does it always have to be about you?

Don't ask me about Fentanyl.
Don't tell me not to dwell.

Don't minimize my loss.
My boy is not better off dead.

For once, let's say it like it is:

He did not pass away.
He died.

There is no plan.
Don't say he is at peace.

Silence is good. A hug.
Tell me you have no words.

Or tell me stories of that summer
he rode the bulls in Ogden,

all that life tightly in his grip.

for K.S-B.

Cruel Choices

When my husband's two grown daughters are in town, the three of them go to the movies, or play pool. Share dinner every night. Stay out late. I haven't seen my stepdaughters since my son's funeral in 2007. When people ask, I say nice things about the girls, as if we had a relationship. When people ask if I have children I change the subject. Or I lie, and say no. Or sometimes I put them on the spot and tell them yes, but he died. They look aghast and want to know what happened. Then I have to tell them about the cancer. Sometimes, when the older daughter, his favorite, is in town, and she and my husband are out together night after night, I wonder what it would be like if that was me, and my boy, if life was fair, and, rather than my husband having two children and I, none, we each had one living child. His choice which one to keep. Lately when people ask, I want to lie and say yes, my son is a basketball coach; he married a beautiful Iranian model with kind eyes, and they live in London with their twin girls who visit every summer; the same twins his girlfriend aborted with my blessing when my son was eighteen, deemed too young for fatherhood, and everyone said there would be all the time in the world.

NOTE: "Overdose" received a Honorable Mention, at Beyond Baroque Poetry Contest, 2019, Judged by Diane Seuss.

"Cruel Choices" was first published in *ASKEW*, 2016, and nominated for the Pushcart Prize, 2017. Winner, Pangolin Review Poetry Contest, and nominated again for the Pushcart Prize in 2018 by *Pangolin Review*.

MARY FITZPATRICK

Basho's Death

not turning, standing still
the snow turning his black hair white
suspended in a bronze gong's
chime not turning
phrases in his mind but letting the notes alight
and write their own lines; seasons turn; standing
in his summer hut
all night grasshoppers churn their tune
Basho writes by the harvest moon's
light; then
not standing still but turning
on highest mountain top he sees
the red carp sun straddle
east and west   turning to catch
its either light standing
in Fuji's red snow while tiny boats
drift below; when the snows melt turning
his muddy feet to riverbanks / plum blossoms
turning in the warm breezes light
with spring, Basho not answering
the call to another cup of plum
wine Basho stands unsteady in a tiny boat,
turns it to moon's broad reflection on the pond
leaning over to kiss it and he's gone

NOTE: First published in *Poet & Critic*, Vol. XIII, No. 3, 1982.

Sweet are the Uses of Adversity

> Sweet are the uses of adversity
> Which, like the toad, ugly and venomous,
> Wears yet a precious jewel in its head.
>   – William Shakespeare

Sweet are the uses of adversity — the office
culture I have grown around, the
strategic plan, draft document, political
message meant to motivate — a skill,
a skein of words I have grown
as an appendage, developed skin around.
Sweet are the uses of adversity — provide
Jesuit, Franciscan, community, university:
the education I had to my children.
Sweet are the uses of adversity — the mate
for twenty years, a skein
of months, laughter, jokes, sorrow, bitterness between us and I
have pits and fissures and blooms and growth
I've grown skin around to stay.
Sweet are the uses of adversity: the modern
whizz, car chase, crammed calendar, lack of peace, the pace
a price to pay for all we have — far from want, we will not starve.
Sweet are the uses of adversity as used
by the hopeful who alit
at Jamestown, Plymouth, any yard
where they planted food and buried
their young, their many dead. A certain determination
swelled; they stayed. And I
— another pair of hands, another hauler
of the great barge forward —
see the head of land, hear sloshing waves,
know my part of the coarse, warty flesh, intent
on that jewel glint.

      NOTE: First published in *Agenda*, Vol. 41. Nos. 3-4, Winter 2005.

MICHAEL C. FORD

A Get-well Card

>To Laurel Ann Bogen

we
have a good idea, Laurel Ann!
whenever you get real down and
sad and flippy and gloomy and
wig'd out and your whole head feels
like the Hindenburg making you feel
like you just want to crash in New Jersey,

why
not pretend all poets in Los Angeles
named Laurel Canyon after you: okay,
but for an assortment of alienated human
beings, it's a crappy canyon full of post
hippie love heads, secular humanists, a

few
reactionary corporate criminals with fat
wallets, an unwholesome variety of
me-generation burnouts; but I know most
LA poets would have the best intention:

holding
one of their own in high esteem; besides,
think about what pigeons in Buffalo, New
York do to the statues at Lafayette Square!

you
see, Laurel Ann, it's really not so terrible to
be able to move around: turning into some

monumental
petrified memory could be just another stone
drag.

JOYCE FUTA

Her Death

It wasn't an answer, it was a question.
It wasn't simple, but dark and teeming.
Like tv detectives, we thought about it,
reconstructed timelines, conversations, events.
The links were there,
everything and nothing made any sense.
Our thoughts ranged wildly depending on the hour,
whether it was gray or bright as the tropics,
what friend we just talked to and whether we wept.
Who could have stopped her vision of fate.
How the seed grew to take over her mind.

Sometimes it seemed simple: it was just too much.

But it wasn't simple, never an answer.
The question echoes as it moves into the past.
lost in caves
we tunnel through grief

  trying to remember your light
  those days in the years
  you walked with us

Kumquat Marmalade

My sister and I slice a huge mound of kumquats for marmalade, a tedious, time consuming task; each tiny fruit has seeds we must tease out with the tip of a knife. One could go nuts doing this alone, but we pass the time chatting about friends, sons, the awful daily news. Twelve jars of orange jellies with little bright haloes of rind will be our reward.

We start to talk about movies. Suddenly we are caught in the familiar senior struggle to remember someone's name, this time an actress we have loved in many roles. We catalog facts we know about her – she played an artist in that movie with whatshisname ... and X's sister in a film set in San Francisco – was she nominated for that? Finally, my sister says she gives up and rinses her hands to google. When she returns with the name, we slap our numbskulls.

slippery seeds of memory
we leave drama behind
and enter the age of comedy

WILLIAM SCOTT GALASSO

Halcyon Days

When I, in youth's morning bore no strain of time,
the world lay open; sky wide, sea deep, elegant green
each tree under dappled sun, each blade of grass was mine,
and birds sang songs mom had no words for, though
she sang so well they sometimes stopped to listen

Or later, hot with summer's sand beneath feet,
mimicked a young seal in wave's curl,
bathed in foam, salt on skin, knew no time
but my own, hungered for nothing but to breathe and be

Or beheld leaves fire fall quilting woods,
hunted newts in creeks behind my house,
small feet traipsing through skunk cabbage acres,
in a tic-tac-toe of trails

Or in winter waged war with snowballs
and sped down white hills virginal, glistening,
pale days, pewter skies, I, pink-cheeked and frozen
sadness then was a rare visitor, soon forgotten,
life's trials fit my size, could be endured

School tallied my waking hours,
and each night birthed a host of dreams,
I became the heroes I read about,
yet dew dies in the meadow, ice forms,
and fireflies in a jar go still

May Day manna
aloe to zinnia blaze
after a drizzle
birdsong freshens air
gladdens my heart

      twenty-twenty
      sign of the times
      FOR SALE

        one breath
        the difference between
        I am and I was

JERRY GARCIA

While Walking the Dog Last Evening

I saw a falling star,
its tail so long,
its head so black,

surely it must rest this morning
in a neighbor's backyard,
blackened rock, warm to the touch,
conspicuous on a thick bed
of blue grass.

If it struck like the truth
it could be the famous Boson
and if it had not been honest,
the prayers of many
would nod as they hold on to tomorrow
while the rest of us scramble
to keep the day intact.

Sometimes, what is visible in the black,
like reflected branches
and multi-galaxies of matter,
would support belief in substance,
while to others
the flickering sky expresses
the Divine.

JOHN GUZLOWSKI

Refugees

We came with heavy suitcases
made from wooden boards by brothers
we left behind, came from Buchenwald
and Katowice and before that
Lwów, our mother's true home,

came with our tongues
in tatters, our teeth in our pockets,
hugging only ourselves, our bodies
stiff like frightened ostriches.

We were the children in ragged wool
who shuffled in line to eat or pray
or beg anyone for charity.

Remembering the air and the trees,
the sky above the Polish fields,
we dreamt only of the lives waiting
for us in Chicago and St. Louis
and Superior, Wisconsin

like pennies
in our mouths.

Thanksgiving Day Poem

My people were all poor people,
the ones who survived to look
in my eyes and touch my fingers
and those who didn't, dying instead

of fever, hunger, or even a bullet
in the face, dying maybe thinking
of how their deaths were balanced
by my birth or one of the other

stories the poor tell themselves
to give themselves the strength
to crawl out of their own graves.

Not all of them had this strength
but enough did, so that I'm here
and you're here reading this poem
about them. What kept them going?

Maybe something in the souls
of people who start with nothing
and end with nothing, and in between
live from one handful of nothing
to the next handful of nothing.

They keep going--through the terror
in the snow and the misery
in the rain--till some guy pierces
their stomachs with a bayonet

or some sickness grips them, and still
they keep going, even when there
aren't any rungs on the ladder
even when there aren't any ladders.

CHARLES HARMON

The Joy of Cooking

I have tears in my eyes
But not from cutting onions
I'm laughing out loud
But not from jokes in my cookbook
Oil is sizzling and hot
But my pan remains empty
Not all the cooking wine
Makes it into the pot

I want to cook for you
I want you in my kitchen
My spice box is exploding
Hot chili peppers set hearts on fire
Curry burns holes in souls
Lips blister from sampling salsa
So sweet and sour

What strange alchemy transforms
Such simple ingredients into life?
Miracle food, magical energy source
Gives strength to go on, for
Neither Woman nor Man
Can live by bread alone

We both need something more
Something hearty that endures
That sticks to Adam's ribs and also Eve's —
A great big serving
Of passion and romance.

I'm dishing that up
With a chef's flair for cuisine

Words of love to nourish
Hungry hearts and thirsty souls
It's hot and spicy and ready…
Are you hungry too?
Care to join me?

NOTE: First published in *Spectrum 4:* "2016's Top Ten San Gabriel Valley Poets, April; *Altadena Poetry Review* 2017; *Prism Review*, Spring 2006; Winner, 2006 "Winner-Take-All" SGVPQ Hollywood Poetry Contest

LLOYD HITT

A Shadow

It seemed,
in a way

That at the same time,
and at no time
I was a child

Yes,
it's clear

There were children's games,
sleds and bicycles too
But where was I?
 To be a child
to be free

To dream like a child,
to laugh and cry
is to explore and defy

Children are
the way they are

To see shadows
on a tinted mirror

I understood — I knew not,
the excitement of risk

Only not to disappoint
only
To be the shadow.

Curiosity

Why are you there?
Are you curious,
      do you care?
I'm curious.
      Why lay you there?

You're alone you say,
and you're satisfied
      things be as they may.
I'm curious.
      No dragons to slay?

Shades are drawn.
The room is dark.
      No thoughts to spawn.
I'm curious.
      Are you gone?

A tiny voice outside the door.
"Grandma are you there?"
      Your feet hit the floor,
I'm curious.
      Why do spirits soar?

Light shines thru open space.
"I love you Grandma."
      From a tiny face.

I'm curious.
      Is this your place?

Brown eyes glow.

"I'm glad you've waited, Grandma."
        She stands in a pink bow.

I'm curious.
        There's much to know.

Our Journey

Walk with me for a little while,
on unmarked lanes we will travel,
        you and I.

Talk to me for a little while,
tell me of love and doubt. Transcend what is real,
        tell me your story.

Sit by me for a little while,
hold my hand and remember the quiet moments
        of so little time.

Sing to me for a little while
your song of life and I will understand
        how rare life is.

Look with me at the lights below
as we ascend together, the stars our beacon,
        you and I, for just a little while.

NOTE: The three poems first published in *The Earth Time*, 2019.

LOIS P JONES

Red Horse

No one understood this blood run
to the moon, this blaze

of you, red horse in a swollen sky.
How you turned loose

like a fistful of fire ants.
How your temper could burn

a field when there was too much
to drink. There were days we'd spread

the blanket on the grasses
near the sycamores and let the desert

air run through us,
let the sage burn our nostrils

as we sipped a silky rioja.
A wine you liked to translate,

as you decoded everything beautiful.
Your lips full and slightly curled

siempre, siempre: jardin de mi agonia,
tu cuerpo fugitivo para siempre,

always, always: garden of my last breath,
your body escaped forever,

Lorca in his red shoes
lighting our tongues, lifting

our hips until the sun
turned poppy and burst.

GEORGIA JONES-DAVIS

Monumental Dog

Where is the dog the Soviets
shot into space in 1957?
Where is Laika tonight?
Her bones could be sailing overhead,
a satellite of the cold war
stuck in the traffic of the commuting sky.
Experts now content
she died of overheating
within hours of launch
because her R-J sustainer failed
to separate from the payload.
Laika died,
the rest of us believe,
an orbiting, kenneled cosmonaut,
a terrified dog star,
night and day chasing past her,
the moon escaping fast as a cat.
She howled, I am the only dog
circling the campfire of the world,
lonesome as a wolf
in the prehistoric shadows.

On the sixth day
her breath evaporated;
she starved and froze in her capsule
as the human sounds she recalled--
"Moya malishka, moya Laylika" --
receded in her ears
with the memory of meat
and Kremlin bells only a dog can hear.
Laika was mailed into space,
a letter never answered,
a missal to the gods of the future.
To please him she submitted

to her handler's velvet-voiced commands,
the same voice that whispered her name.
She thrilled to the clammy, cushiony hands
that stroked her fur
even as they strapped her in.

After the Storm

Last night ended at the water's edge,
on an unbroken boardwalk,
above a lapping, tranquil ocean.
I followed a trail down the mountain
until there was nothing but blackberries,
nothing but their alluring darkness
between me and the sea.

There was no turning back.
I was going to live in a new house,
a secretive house
that stood beside my own,
a house with a view of the bay.
The house with shutters was painted
brilliantly as a parrot,
orange and apricot and jade.

The people who lived there,
a widow with a young son,
were going away to somewhere
tropical and foreign.
Those who move out of a house
and those who move in
never quite become friends,

even if they have lived side by side
for as many years as it takes
to never get to know each other,
and the rickety fence that separates
their gardens
has fallen down in the wind.

C.E. JORDAN

possum garden

this living-space
out of doors, by
day, glows, shift-
ing its spotlights.
But by night to
night I found
all the familiar
places hording their
own kind of light.

Like my white x-
mas lights, strung
common, are now
as good as
steaming
searchlights, making
my pagoda's ceiling
its own Hollywood
premier
and the latest
possum waddling
across the red
carpet, shining
his day-glo mime-
masque right straight
in my direction. Creatures

tame and not, natural
for the most part, go
phosphorescent, and
blink tidings from
white patches

here and there. And
Vinca and periwinkle-shaped
wheels of light,
teeming stars
in white crockery
whiter and still no
moon. Then

the sounds like heat
seem to rise and
float dismembered
in the semi-darkness.
Voices badgering, more
wild things whining low.
And crickets, I'm sorry,
but you have to hear
this tiny, squeaking
chorus, hallelujahs
& noir plots this
night, growing home-
made stories &
third man types
shadow-hopping,
wild life out
here.

MANDY KAHN

The Tour Guide

I followed the German tour guide
through the hulking old basilica.

He told the group (or so I guessed),
indicating high and low:

This is where the wind begins.

This is where the childhoods of a thousand
martyrs live, untouched.

Wood grain in these pews still curls
to likenesses of patron saints.

Window-holes are cut the breadth
of human souls, when loosed.

Dark paint in the frescoes is crushed ants.
White paint is light.

Leaves and fauna long extinct are rendered
in the porticoes. See that goat
with antlers? Gone from life,
but captured here.
(Hold your breath and it bows its head.)
(Reach towards the ceiling and sigh, and it sighs.)

Worth two times the value of the Bulgar Sea
is that old bell.

(When younger priests
would ring it,
the nuns were warned to shield their hearts.)

He said far more
I can't recall

and when I tried to pay him,
he spurned my coins, saying, in German,
What good is money,
my child, to the wind?

The Everyday

Old friends, old loves, I celebrate
the day-to-day you've found: the favored cup,
the dog, the child, the husband, wife—
the hat rack by the door, the bowl of keys,
the chair in sun,
weekends with your omelets made
just right. You graduated into
the encyclopedic pleasures of the everyday,
that brighter vision—
the sharp phantasmagoria you enter
when you watch your child through sprinkler water:
that moving prism.

Didn't I always tell you, lover, roommate,
there were portals by the dishtowels?

                    You think you left your dreams.

You've entered
the Basilica of the Present
by its common causeway.

This, your striving earned.

MINA KIRBY

When I Was Me

When I was me
in bow ribbons
and kittens
and ice cream
I saw spring melt
into a buttercup
and heard symphonies
in wind-wafted trees

When I was me
in turquoise
and breezes
and cartwheels
I ran up the mountain
the sun warm on my face
and caught sparkles
in a flowing brook

When I was me
lacy
and pink
and vibrant
I was in love
wanting togetherness
for every minute
and for all time

Where did I go
that long-haired
lemon-scented
idealistic girl
who thought

she could absorb
all the tastes
in the universe

What prickly troubles
put obstacles
in my path
changed starry-eyed into ordinary
or did I
caught in whispers
of shifting clouds
just let *me* slip away

Perhaps one day
when soft rains turn to sunshine
and flowing water
pours over hard rocks
in a small place inside myself
I will find clothed with soft smooth silk
in purple and crimson and gold
the new me

and learn to love her too

A Special Place

It is warm here
Golden rays of sunshine
brighten green fields
fragrant with yellow flowers
The air sparkles
with hums of bees

and chirps of soaring birds
A gentle breeze ruffles my hair
In the distance
are sounds of an ocean's roar
as it splashes against rocks

I could be here
yesterday
tomorrow
and today
I could be here in the sun
and the softly falling rain
in the cheerful daylight
and in the velvety darkness

I could be here with you
feel the warmth of your hand in mine
talk until the moon goes down
and stars sparkle in the night sky
We could walk
for miles and miles
absorbing the beauty
surrounding us

Or
I could be here alone
a little sadder
but content
as perhaps
some day
I will
cloaked in sunshine
remembering you

ANDREW KOLO

America of an Immigrant

The first things which an immigrant
notices through the windows
of a Boeing 747 is the sharp
needles of Manhattan
and the Statue of Liberty
standing right by it with
a serious countenance.

In the middle of the window lie
green carpets of the Des Moines farms.
From the horizon rays of fourteen carat
California sun's blur
and in the fog on the right
atomic explosions in Nevada.

He also sees millionaires
and the less wealthy
And the saints from Lynchburg, Virginia,
and finally his view from the window is
obliterated by Coca-Cola…
bursting from the clouds.

Dinosaurs

Four dinosaurs like
four mountains
angrily break palm trees
They rush through the boulevard
straight toward La Brea Tar Pits

into the Museum of Ethnography.
The bones of their brothers'
from millions of years ago
are resting here in plastic boxes

President with his speech
to the nation tries the microphone:
1, 2, 3…
Conservatives and liberals
are ready to applaud his special plan.

Dinosaurs break museum walls.
Clasp their brothers' bones.
Hug them…and…cry

Garden of Eden

In the Garden of Eden brightly colored
flowers and bushes never cease blooming
and never knew winter.
The fig tree belongs to you - my dearest
and the olive one - to me.
Make yourself comfortable
in their aromatic shade.

In the tangled branches snake is hissing softly.
Under an apple tree Adam and Eve, embracing.
I give you sons and daughters – she whispers
tucking him into an animal fur coat.
This delicious fruit called an apple
can only make you stronger – my beloved.

   The first snowflakes are beginning to fall
   upon the flowery Garden of Eden
   like the first sins.

DEBORAH P KOLODJI

white marble
I am small at the feet
of Lincoln

      floating purple--
      my daydreams follow
      the water hyacinth

highway
of sleeping towns
the milky way

      settling the estate
      empty gum wrappers
      in her purse

the scarf
she never finished
brown pine needles

      morning tidepools
      a hermit crab tries on
      the bottle cap

winter sea
the rise and fall
and fall

      a caterpillar's progress
      across the fallen leaf
      jet lag

moon flower
a love letter
to Captain Kirk

      LA traffic
      our lady of the perpetually
      late

our history
written in rock
desert lavender

MARIKO KITAKUBO

Borderless Prayer

1
rhythm of
dripping water
midnight--
when did it
turn to crimson?

2
overseas events
are cancelled
but our hope
won't die young
rainbow above the ocean

3
finding
a tiny light...
when
I rise up against
the disappointment

4
let's not
search for someone
to blame
we were born
to help each other

5
making
a spring wreath
of pansy
yellow, purple, white...
survived winter

6
without
color, language,
nationality...
another world
in the reflection of water

7
go back
to god's territory
like when
we were born
to see honesty

8
before
our endless
sleep
we can spread
our wings, again

9
tears
are meaningless
use the time
for pure
borderless prayer

SHARMAGNE LELAND-ST. JOHN

Bruna Vieira gathers flowers

Bruna Vieira gathers flowers in her garden
she dreams of wildflowers but
chooses sunflowers instead
she's smart she knows they'll last the longest
she'll cut the stems tall, put sugar in the water
and hope they'll still be beautiful
when he comes to visit on Sunday

in her dreams she's dressed in hymns
not jeans and a blue and white striped pullover
she dances for the flowers and calls them Girasol
as they nod their sunshine heads
in the blue and white Meissen vase
where she has carefully arranged them
with their stems cut at an angle

she spins and her red hair is a furore of flames
leaping and licking the scented air behind her
she has *adagio* and *lento*
tattooed in curlicues' on opposite ankles
to remind her of the tempo of the dance
and the rhythm of her life
in black ink a flutter of sparrows
dot her left wrist ...
as she reaches out to caress the flowers
one of the sparrows flies away

NOTE: Pushcart Prize Nominee, 2019.

She dreams...

she lies down beside him
her dreams projected
on her forehead
in monochrome
he sees her through
sepia eyes.

she dreams
ballerina dreams
she dreams of locomotives
and crashing waves
she dreams of footprints
vanishing like the prairie
she dreams of rain
she dreams of a lover.

she dreams he will
watch her forehead
and know exactly what she wants
she dreams of a tender man
his warm breath on the nape of her neck
she dreams of crickets
and a stranger with kiss-able lips
she dreams of archipelagos

he unbuttons every button
on her blue silk blouse, slowly,
it falls from her shoulders
and slips away
she wonders about moonbows
she dreams of black roses
and he whispers softly as she sighs

JAMES LEVIN

A.M. Ride

Pedaling on the bike,
early morning stars
study your behavior.
You power through
chilly air,
shift gears,
breathe in
nuanced ways.

You are perspiring,
panting
to the
thump thumping
of your knees.

You feel
increased resistance
up the rise,
then cruise
to a halt.

You dismount,
stretch,
alone
and fulfilled.

WAYNE ALLEN LEVINE

No Way Back

I needed to get out today, after being
Sequestered for nearly a
Decade inside that granite mountain,
Searching for the ever-elusive diamond mine.

Now the world is asking me for
Everything, and I wish only to comply.
And it doesn't matter where I
Left off yesterday – or where I
Imagine or pretend to begin today.

Maybe I'll move to New Mexico
And let my beard grow . . . allow
My gray-brown whiskers to soften
My fleshy marble chin, and dance
With some of the other artists of my day.
Maybe I'll climb to the top of a
Sacred mesa – watch a sunset through
The eyes of a brand new man
And permit my thoughts to fall like quiet rain.

Then, I'll dry my emotions with the
Open end of a one-time-only rainbow –
Catch salmon in a bubbling brook
And cook my lucid dreams a little longer.
Maybe I'll stain an empty canvas with
Unstrained honey, ancient sand, and
Half a glass of elderberry wine –

Then carve a bow from a willing branch –
A bendable cypress or pliable oak, mold
My arrows from hardened stardust,
And fashion tips from skipping stones . . .
Maybe I'll shoot strait, this time? Hit my target
Dead-center, then dance home again, stopping

Along the way to see, and smell, and savor all
The roses, daisies, tulips, and erupting wildflowers.

And if all the crumbs I scattered along
The way have been feasted upon by
Tiny birds that never learned, though
Always knew exactly how to pray . . .
I won't feel the least bit lost – knowing
All the while that there never was a way of getting back.

Only This

It was only a dream. It was only a fantasy.
It was only a wish. It was only
My buoyant imagination running
Away with me – running away from me.
It was only a grandiose daydream –
While searching for guidance at a dizzying pace.
It was only another euphoric flash
In the pan that amounted to nothing.
It was only my naivety
Attempting to protect me –
A hollow echo in the guise of an opening song.
It was only a matter of time before
My fascination with reverie would
Be abruptly interrupted by reality –
Wherein, the passive-aggressive illusion of
Logic runs roughshod over my unexpressed passions.
It was only a thought, only an idea, it was only
My destiny begging, pleading, needing to be lived.
It was only a moment,
Which lasted an hour
That stretched into a day,
Which turned into a lifetime.
It was only the elongated shadow of a brave little boy,
Creating the welcomed illusion of a full-grown man.
It was only another anonymous poet –
Spitting grape seeds and soliloquy into the wind.

STEPHEN LINSTEADT

Saint-Rémy de Provence

A wale of rock jumps out of the land
and freezes above the earth;
the backdrop to "Starry Night"
painted close to where green bathed
the artist's vision in a yellow
       tainted room.
The scent of Languedoc
still warm about your neck.

Thunder uncoils over the night.

Rain on my umbrella

drops of deep mystery. Madness in May
only warm iris blossoms understand.

Their light whispers
and won't hold still.

You can't complain that I'm singing
     this is an asylum.

And where are the human beings
who once lived in the olive groves?

We were compelled to keep our distance
     from the chapel.

Pigeons cooed then waited
for the echo to reverberate
off its stained-glass walls.

ELLINE LIPKIN

My Parents Meet at *La Grande Place*
Brussels, Belgium

He sits in a corner café, waiting for the girl
as he looks up at the tarnished domes
that crowd the broad shoulders of buildings.
Tiny streets break off at corners like veins,
bleeding as streams of people course in and out.
Again feeling a slight tremor, he thinks,
'it's as they told me: the pages of history.'

Shop windows line the square, decorated
with endless patterns of ancient lace.
Spinsters working at their spools,
'the last of a dying breed,' he thinks,
their longing patterned into an intricacy
that unravels if only the smallest thread is pulled.

He knows that behind him in Brooklyn
his mother is setting out her good tablecloth.
She will study the black and white photographs,
edges cut crisp as the scalloped *gaufres* he eats.
The phrases he learns seem too small for his yearning,
his broad accent breaking the delicate china plates
of French words he wants to caress.

But no one had told him about the loneliness,
how some dawns would rise with no break
from the black of night, the day so shrouded
he wondered how planes could get through,
when no reference, no Rilke, no grand extrapolation
could keep the grey from creeping over each white wall,
blank as the map once laid out to chart the New World.

Limoncello
Boussu, Belgium

We drank limoncello
late into the June night
settled underneath the green
canopy just set up at the
edge of my uncle's backyard.

The grass had been stroked
into neat lines, stripes of clean
carpet he made sweeping his living
room lawn, the forest's near edge
a frayed cuff he couldn't cut off.

Sheltered beneath the night's dark
arch we ringed the cedar table, close
as the koi swimming in the square
pond cut into the stone, a low well
that held their turning within bounds.

Our voices murmured into the waft
of jasmine, the drift of citronella,
the candles' nimbus a bridge floating
languid talk, mixing our motley tongues
as we each held a glass of the yellow

bitter-sweet and shared the taste
of ripened lemons, a distillate of
sun-scored skin, the viscous glow
within each glass like a light to
the past, each child once a heat-baked

streak of whitened blond spinning past
a fence or gate. We tasted memory's
liqueur, settled from the years' dank *cave*,
made a *réunion* with each cup's citrus
spice, silence joining us like a pulse.

B.D. LOVE

Declan IV

I hold a photograph of you sitting in a box
Half-full of trim from the ancient pepper tree
Whose leaves would choke the eaves and drives and vex
The neighbor lady, who pleaded for the penalty

Of downing — this for a being much of her time.
She'd pass, pure white, beneath the "dirty" limbs.
"There's a fungus among us," my mom would chime
By way of warning. Indeed, there was. Death has her hymns.

But here you are, roots in the mulch, your face
Courting the camera's heart. The shutter clicks
And off you go to sniff all crones and grace
All trees with piss before a smaller box

Arrives to collect the last of the dust to fall.
Some old limbs creaked that night. I heard their call.

NOTE: First published in *Nimrod*

RICK LUPERT

Heat

It is nine in the morning and already too hot.
Ninety degrees in the San Fernando Valley

It is truly a *dog day* of summer.
At ten-thirty in the morning it is two hundred degrees.

Hot enough to keep a pie comfortably warm,
so when you are ready, you could scoop

vanilla ice cream on top.
Serve immediately.

At one in the afternoon
it is six hundred degrees.

Hot enough to cook a family of four,
though certain laws request you don't.

At four in the afternoon
most of the Earth's surface has burned away.

I'm writing this underneath the
last remaining palm tree

in a place as far away from the equator
as one could be.

A gaggle of deceased penguins
stares at me *wantingly*.

Nine o-clock in the evening
I go to bed. It is too hot to be awake anymore.

Probably fifteen hundred degrees.
I'd check the news for tomorrow's potential

but they are gone. I'm going to sleep
until the ice monsters come

until they develop clothing especially for this
until the breaking of the fall.

Animal Hospitality

I can tell which cat is walking through my house
by the sounds its paws make as they come
into contact with the wood floors.

At one in the morning when I finally arrive at my bed
Cleo walks in. She is the oldest cat. Not in the world,
just in the house. You can barely hear her since we took her claws

nine years ago. She propels herself to the bed
like a kite. No sound. No bounce. She makes herself.
comfortable. At five in the morning she will purr.

I'd tell you the name of my next cat is Tigger,
but then you would judge me.
He walks in like a pony wearing tap shoes.

If I make even the slightest audible sound or motion
he will rush to the bed and lick any visible skin
of mine he can find. I am okay with this.

Our third cat is larger than a moose. He'd come to
the bed but he can't find room. His breathing is
louder than the president's helicopter.

He will cry for his breakfast with the imperative
of Vietnam. *You're running a zoo* my friend once said
to which I replied. *Let me show you the Chinese*

water dragon and the frog. Did I tell you I tried to keep
a bird alive that I'd found outside? It didn't make it.
Did I tell you about the caterpillar I killed?

RADOMIR LUZA

Tall Oak Trees with Gray, Flowing Moss

There is no reason
There is no time

There is no language
There is no rhyme

There is only New Orleans
In its emerald skies
Strawberry highs
Bayou breath
Beignet bet

Only this town
Surging in the light
Singing at dusk
Banging big bucks

American miracle
Southern Jezebel
Dreaming at dawn
With considerable brawn
Leaning into vanilla clouds
Polluted lake
River needing rake

Crescent City without pity
Stretching into Gordon Liddy

Pure enough to meet any goal
Language and salient soul

New Orleans, my brother
New Orleans, my sister

Weeping under oval moon
Interstate swoon
St Charles Avenue streetcar in June

World not made for your sort of parade
Universe too sore to admire your azure door

Not wise enough to respect your European roots
Heart beating above French Quarter breast
Curve ball into swaggering magenta Magnolias
Sweating onto humid chest

Please Big Easy
Do not give in to the sleazy
Instead find cafe of mocha and bean
Lonesome dove and the ghost of James Dean
On other side of love

Driving Downtown
To the Superdome
Where the Saints moan

Crossing the River
On an old steamboat like Mark Twain
Just to keep sane on
Your Sweltering Summer afternoons
Crazy old town

Keep the Gumbo coming
Let the Po-Boys sizzle

I will return decade after decade
To taste your rainy drizzle

SUZANNE LUMMIS

Flour, Eggs, Milk, Baking Powder, Salt and God

O Best Beloved, tell me, if you know, why —
the world over — when that woman bending
toward the griddle, toward heat pushing through
the a.m. chill, turns up a soft brown impression
of an unshaven face surrounded by loose hair, why
does she always think it's Jesus?

And her proud, abruptly ennobled husband agrees,
and her chattering neighbors — It's him!
A miracle! — as if they'd know that face anywhere.
Beloved, take this instruction: don't believe all you hear.
It could be Juan Ponce de Leon looking much
as he did when he surveyed the fresh-growing land

he'd name Pascua Florida, pointing — according
to legend — his sharp little beard toward the Waters
of Bimini, the "Fountain of Youth," searching
not finding, but even his beard hard at work. Or —

it could be his fellow Spaniard and relation,
Rodrigo Ponce de Leon, The Marquez of Cadiz!

But if the outline of gently singed batter describes
a head with luxurious gypsy curls and the artfully
shaped beard and moustache of a man so careful
with his looks he can afford to be careless with women,
oh that's Lindsey Buckingham! You know,
lead singer for Fleetwood Mac, just as he looked

that madcap summer in L.A. when everyone
was sleeping with everyone and getting divorced,
and all of them, John and Christine McVie,

Mick Fleetwood, Stevie Nicks, inhaling, breathing
cocaine, until it drifted from their garments
like the sprinklings of Disney fairies.

Damn, he was a handsome man.
Those pancakes don't do him justice.

But can we blame them, the folks who trudge home
each Sunday from the market lugging bags of onions,
potatoes, slabs of meat, flour — enough for one week —
eggs. They want Mystery, who doesn't? Sanctity.
A visitation. They want it for breakfast.

This morning, Beloved, while you lay still
asleep, the batter dreamed against the deep
cast iron griddle, against the bluing flames.
I cooked a flat cake, then a second, a third, and,
no, it was not the first one I prized, the one
with the secretive smile, nor the one after that,

whose eyes followed me around the room
as I searched for the tub of butter whip.
I enjoyed most that one on the bottom, the last
and the least, unleavened, the truly mysterious
pancake, the faceless one, with no expression at all.

NOTE: First published in *Plume*.

Answer like a House Burning Down

How does the thin-furred doe, fox,
how does the cougar
run in the night chill—sting
in the air, cold banking in from the east,
East wind, massive female moon
lighting the frost-tipped leaves?
I've always wondered.
Fellow insomniac, Newton cat,
sits on the porch keeping
his eye on the road, that marble
eye. His face wears a comfortable look.
Why isn't he cold? I am,
was, always since my extreme
youth, that shadowy
tunnel through snow leading
from the lodge door
to the surface of the knowable
world. Years later—"Oh it's part
of my ensemble," I'd say, when
the host asked for my coat.
I have not changed but now
the change has come on me:
tropical blood storm, furred
heat on the skin. So
this late, sixty degrees
and falling, I rise
from the kitchen table, throw
open the door and leave you, not
forever—though the night hits me
like deep water I've dropped
suddenly into and find I can breathe.
I'm no romantic.
I never believed in a knowledge
borne only by woman
till now. In the body's last

ungovernable flaring up before
scorching out, I walk for blocks
and the dark stays big enough
to cool off in — and the sky, too,
with its burden of space,
its chilly secret of the infinite.
Back home you turn under
the bulb light
as if unwinding the puzzled air, man
with all the right questions.
I am the answer to one of them,
an answer like a house burning down.
Cold pavement, cold mauve-tinted air.
I know how the ferret can slip
over frozen ground, and the wolverine
and the wolverine's prey,
mid-winter, mid
two a.m. hour, in the far
hills, stark
outskirt of fields.

NOTE: First published in *The Drunken Boat*.

Not There

O Best Beloved, in this dream
I'm trying to recall a word,
a sort of heat-flushed hallucination.
What is it?! This bit of chalk won't
do—cracks in my fingers or goes black
as the board I test its strength on.
The group turns restive,
disrespectful. "Class," I challenge,
"what's this when it occurs
on desert sand? I l u s i o n...."
The letters hold a moment then sink
back as into shadowed water,
night sky. Behind me, the chipped
noise of speech rattles around
in itself, but no one is speaking to me.
And now I awake. I'm awake but still
can't remember, know nothing. Oh what
are you, what is your name?
You light pricked by Saguaro thorns,
light towards which the near-dry
wells weep up, dry heat, the mind's
thirst and hunger of the tongue,
I have traveled this far on
sore feet to worship at your cold,
unhaunted, ineffable
      altar—
monsoon moon song mir-
thing mirror mere
roar   Mirage

NOTE: First published in *Malpais Review*.

SHAHE MANKERIAN

Writer's Block at Father's Grocery Store

Coarse coffee grinds took the color
of Medusa's hair. A pound of garbanzo

weighed less than Nabokov's Lolita.
A bag of pita felt softer than Juliet's

pillow before suicidal Romeo. I wrote
countless villanelles on paper bags

before stuffing them with cans of dolma,
bottled rose water, and pouches

of Aleppo pepper. I thought I saw
the Karamazov Brothers tasting Kalamata

olives. Sometimes I sat on cardboard
boxes full of fava beans and daydreamed

about Anne Sexton. I couldn't write
because Father called me back to work.

Madame Bovary wanted two pounds
of French ham sliced thinner than lined paper.

NOTE: Published in *The Indian River Review* / April 2016.

MIRJANA N. RADOVANOV MATARIĆ

Land of Canyons and Arches

Saturated with grandiose beauty I cannot absorb more
at the top of endless horizons from which is best to embrace all.
At an elevation of seven thousand feet
two ravens sit and watch us,
perched on a fence formed from ageless limbs of an old local tree
grayed and washed-out by time and elements
for hundreds of years

The larger obviously male and the smaller, built finer, a female.
They sit there looking at us, the ones who do not belong.

We drove for many miles in our funny moving machine
spewing noise and fumes, yet unable to fly
while they soar high into the crystal blueness of the sky,
over pink and red rocks masterfully sharpened by water and ice,
hoodoos line the Grand Staircase
their sediment filling old waterbeds.

The ravens' eyes not curious, not afraid
just sharp and wisely knowing.
When we leave, they will stay here where they belong.
We will drive down, they will fly up.

As I ventured closer to the edge to embrace the vast majesty
I saw the smaller following probably because
of my jar of mixed nuts
I threw one before her, she quietly picked it
then looked at me as if to say thank you.

The male suddenly swooped in each time I threw a nut to her
he rapidly cut in blocking her picked it up and swallowed fast,
I could not believe my eyes.

The female did not fight over it, not even try. She knew better.
When I stopped after he got more than enough.
He flew off, hopefully satisfied.

The two of us stayed. She did not show greed or even hunger.
I started throwing one after another.
She ate methodically slowly with grace.
There was always that look, like "thank you."
I knew she had enough, but thought she could be a mother,
so, I gave her more. I knew she was grateful but needing to go.
We looked at each other with understanding
and parted as friends.

Near Moab, Utah, 4 December 2014.

Oxymoron

I have always felt an attraction for the oxymoron.
It sounds so good
I see the world as an oxymoron spacious but tight for me;
wonderfully sad and sadly wonderful.
Nothing for me to change since the change is going on anyway,
filled with loneliness in crowds, marriages,
families and corporations.
But love helps.

What about love?
I know it is installed in each of us like chips in a hard drive,
somewhere in our heart or chest and babies show it best
but we do not use it, so we are successfully
and thoroughly loveless and so are others.
The world is a well-structured
Oxymoron.

MARIA ELENA MAHLER

La Machi

Nobody knows her name, only the color of her skin.

If I had a photograph of her face
it would be sepia cracked by the storms over Mapuche land.

Her eyes would be dark stones of lava and
her hair flowing rivers of molten core.

Above Alerce forest, pumas draw the circle.
In my dreams I have seen her chewing *chamico*.

Along Chilean valleys, water runs horizontal
spoiling the virginity of Andean snow, where la Machi

got sweaty under the Araucaria tree.

His *mal de ojo* broke her spell.

Their passion over the still wet moss was all they had
between them.

The impediment to their holy union wasn't the raven
in her hair
but the bonds of duty as *la chamana*:
    forbidden to leave the underworld.

Breaking the sacred law meant certain death
so she quietly gave up her fruit:
    first a boy
    then a girl — my grandmother.

GABRIEL MEYER

A Harvest of Springs Struck by Lightning

I

He washed down the words,
"You think I'm crazy,"
with water,
before he slipped away.

It remained for a lover
but to drain the glass.

II

(She stumbled upon her little sculptor
years later, quite by accident,
curled against a wall
sketching stonework like a child.

He did not look up.

"You've come to apologize, I suppose.")

Still Life, With Lilacs

>   in memoriam Ken Nelson

The ghost of a man in a wicker chair,
Left quite alone.

Shawl sibilant with the sounds
That mammals make
When they sleep in the frozen earth.

Since carnal food has failed him now,
Friends have brought him lilacs to eat
With his eyes.

NAIA

songbird
even the crow in the next tree
listens

      new love . . .
      still some green
      in these autumn leaves

           in those moments
           when all is still and he's sure
           I'm asleep . . .

                the way his lips linger
                upon my bare shoulder

Ghosts Among the Cornflowers

From this place at the edge of a cornflower patch
so wide that it seems as if a great wave poured from the
afternoon sky and liquefied the land . . . from
this place, I begin to wonder. Who planted them?
Who knelt here, tended here, bent and yielded here,
dreamed here? Who planted these cornflowers gone
to seed, to weed, again and again, until this knee-deep
sea of them?

windswept cloud . . .
   in blue ink the apology
      owed since childhood

TOTI O'BRIEN

Of the Palm

I admire the naivety
How she stands among fellow trees
sporting nothing
but a scanty cluster of leaves
in guise of a canopy
as if going to a Victorian ball
in flapper attire
also wearing of course
a feathered hat

Of the palm
I admire the frail nakedness
delicately *osé*
like a dancer's shaved leg
sheathed by nylon hoses

If she dares
intruding the arboreal crowd
without blinking
while so shamefully alien
uncaring of uniforms
she reveals
among sister specimens
exceptional
skills of discipline

How they march in orderly rows
tracing parallels
with their trunks
fastening earth and sky
with thin stitches

How concertedly
at the first puff of wind
they tickle the horizon
as if playing a keyboard
with soft, even touch
whole steps half steps
hand in hand
up and down the scale
facilement

NOTE: First published in *Zingara Poetry*, 7/17/2019

Albino

On her birthday
she dons a platinum
wig. For how long
has she wished
to relinquish her
colors?
Wear her hidden
paleness, revealing
not illness or fading
but a secret self
private yet
statuesque in its smallness
smooth like granite
lip-sealed or
whispering
only speaking
in tongues.

NOTE: First published in *Sunlight Press*, 11/14/2018

CECE PERI

Trouble Down the Road

At the flat top grill, he was all business,
flung raw eggs dead center into the corned beef
hash like a strapping southpaw.

In the alley, with me, he was all ideas.
Said he'd be leaving soon, had a shot back east —
a tryout for the big leagues.

Said his sister would loan him a Buick convertible,
and he'd fill it with malt beer and tuna.
All he needed was a woman to hold

his cat while he drove.
I like animals, I told him. Then I dropped
my cigarette into the dusty clay,

ground it out, slow,
felt the road under my foot.

NOTE: First published in *Luvina: Los Angeles Issue*.

Who Says Bodhisattvas Can't Have Fun?

Kuan Yin, Chinese deity who vowed
to postpone her entrance to paradise
until all become enlightened,

bypasses the stationary cars
on Coney Island's Wonder Wheel
and chooses a swinging one

that dives into a sudden plunge
along snaky iron rails and shoots out
over the spandex-clad, hot dog eating crowds.

Her companion, Hale Makua, Hawaiian
shaman, relishes the salty air rushing
his face. From the Star People, he is

the one who steered the first canoe
to arrive in this world, and will leave
on the last one out.

Their next stop is the Cyclone where they'll sit
in the coveted red front seat of the rickety,
wooden roller coaster, whose first drop

from starry heights has terrified and thrilled riders
for nearly a century. Today they are lucky,
the owner is offering free trips to anyone

brave enough to ride again.

NOTE: First published in *San Diego Poetry Annual*.

A.R. PETERSON

Poem for Augustine

> "...Pass, therefore, beyond the mind of the artist,, so that thou mayest see the everlasting rhythm..."
> Augustine of Hippo, circa 400.

Tonight!
Traffic humming.
Locust trees blooming,
filling the air with scented messengers.

Tingling benediction:
newly watered grass on naked toes,
roughness, sensuousness:
a pendulous frond of birch...
Press against the horny trunk,
listen for the rhythm.

Darkling garden:
bushes full of stirrings
and the willows are not still
but there is no breeze.
Suddenly!
Cat dashes across the lawn.
Someone!
Switches on a light
and the willows dance against it.

The light goes out:
Moonrise, immensity of Space
closes in.
Uncowed, stand erect,
legs splayed, back straight,
arms raised; let fingertips
touch stars.

Here is the rhythm Augustine,
humming, scented, flickering, dashing, rustling, trickling,
extending...
But what is this?
Arms cradling cat,
nostrils flaring to the scent,
ears melding rustles and hums,
eyes caught with the moon in the web of the willows...

Tonight I have no prayers Augustine.

> NOTE: First Published in *Perestroika Poems*, 2012.

The Light That Fails

Any light
that gets too bright
blinds the sight

just as rhyme
gets unsublime
any time
it becomes an end in itself

> NOTE: First Published in *Perestroika Poems*, 2012.

THELMA T. REYNA

Broken Heart Syndrome

There is such a thing,
doctors say—not
the zigzag-split pointy hearts, two
pasted halves on Hallmark cards.
No, docs say, hearts really do fall apart.

Disasters shred our fibers like thieves picking
pockets in broad day. Suddenness of things gone
wrong, small or big,
chip chunks of stamina and strength
from hearts like Greenland's glaciers sliding into
open sea. Our chambers are invaded, locks picked,
thresholds split, so heartbreak can slip in.

Yes, doctors say, there is such a thing.

A violent spat, a gun jabbed in your face. A lover in his mistress'
embrace, caught in your bed. A husband with a bullet in his
head, or found suddenly at dawn, blankets warm but skin cold.
Startling things, ambush-grief, unplanned loss, faith shattered
and tossed. World upended, though brief, can be enough to
cleave your heart.

Yes, doctors say there is such a thing.

No wonder, then, that spouses married long and tight, depart
this world in tandem, or one soon after. No wonder, then, that
when Carrie, princess of galaxies, died sudden, her icon mother,
consumed with grief, followed close. No wonder, then, that
elders in love for life
die days apace.

Yes, not all wounded depart, but they
stumble along, with fluttering hearts, weakened
pulse, leaking valves, raided chambers... puttering
onward, broken heart syndrome and all.

Yes, doctors say there is such a thing.

This is How Grief Goes

> "When we are grieving, people may wonder about us,
> and we may wonder about ourselves."
> —Elisabeth Kubler-Ross*

When loss is swift, when it strikes like a viper in a pot,
blunting hopes and well-laid plans, the hole
that swallows us is bottomless and fierce.

Emptiness unspools like mummy's tape, endless, frayed,
muffling,
gagging, dooming lips and eyes to tombs devoid of words and
light,
stripped of loving hands,
caverns of ululations.

Loss flattens us.
But this is how grief goes.
This is how we sink, to rise,
how brokenness is patched together again,
how despair ultimately defies death.

CINDY RINNE

Places I Belong When the World is Upside Down

I fly past morning glories, pollen, and new moon

Outreach my hand to catch a stars' tail

Physical pain allows me to become vast like a world with four moons

Tarot reading contains lots of swords and says to stop overthinking

My powerful heart bravely grabs myth, nature, and spirit

I co-create with the universe stitcheries and stories

Seeds awaken as roots plow downward in holy ground

Explore Butoh by moving water in the body and disappear like ash

Bow in gratitude to the collaborative gift of a new friend

Guardian goose encourages my quest to legendary places

I join in oneness with others at the apex balancing the chakras

NOTE: Published by *Call and Response: Collaboration at a Distance*, Shoebox PR, 2020.

The Land Owns Me

I.
One day a kestrel visits for the first time and lands near
me. Knows things have changed again. Cannot see,
touch, or smell the ashes of isolation. Other birds join in
the cacophony of sounds – mockingbird, mourning dove,
towhee. A new generation birthed. I hold the raku pot
looking for memories to place inside.

II.
Santa Ana winds blow fierce between gaps in the San
Gorgonio Mountains. I recall this all used to be olive
groves. Ravens still catch air drafts and coyotes travel the
streets like old paths. Wildflowers grab hold anywhere
there is a speck of dirt. Bats flutter in front of my garage
and the unseen owl calls its mate. I
have become the land.

III.
I stand at your roots
Reach out my hands
To touch your smooth
Underbelly where your
Bark has been eaten and
Ask how you are doing
During the virus?
You reply with
Follow the wind song
Gazing straight up
I feel small below
Your vast arms
Full of new spring
Leaves, guardian
Of the charred fields.

SUSAN ROGERS

Longing for October

I looked for you
among leaves
so full of color

they burst
like cherry flames
singing of sap.

I looked for you
in the blood of autumn,
trees warmed by sunfire.

Spinning in the pulse
of maple and beech
anthocyanin sugaring

green veins
as spring sugars
the sky with sakura.

I looked for you
in the chill of autumn,
mountains filling

the sweep of space
with strokes of brilliance
knowing it is both

fire and frost
that paints the tree,
knowing every love

turns to deeper shades
of longing as it rises
into fullness.

You are wind
and water moving
across the face of leaves.

You are the invisible
made visible,
sap rising

until it explodes
in a symphony of light
everywhere I look

in the canopy.

Gratitude

Some days, like yesterday, when the rain falls
the dust that sifts over all things, trees, fence posts, walls
smears black streaks across my car.
But other days, like this morning when it rains
my white car is ultra-white, unmarred,
completely clear of yesterday's stains.
Water drops dance like jewels on its roof,
on the edges of its windshield glass and in my eyes.
The bright air and I seem harmonized.
I drive into this new day clean, lit with proof
of a radiant attitude. The wet leaves tremble and sing
"Thank you, thank you." And I sing back to everything.
The whole world gleams, intensified, imbued
as I shimmer, opening in gratitude.

SHARON RIZK

Coming Up for Air

There will be times
when you may notice
something
missing

remember then
you come from here
seaweed forests crooned
at your arrival

sweetly undulate
each time that you return
you will visit land
pretend

that walking suits you
but know
of something
not alarming wrong

but not precisely right
San Francisco dawn
when her bridge is nestled
in a vagrant cloud

fallen out of formation
to feel its way through
and round girders, cables
veins of traffic

vaguely heard
but not seen and so
the bridge as well
not there

you will come up for air
another sea to wash through you
that turns your blood bright red
when you inhale

and darkens
as it courses through
your body
as if

there were a time continuum
upon which
you could spot yourself
to avoid confusion, disarray

the sense of
something
missing
as you turn and turn

when air becomes unbearable
when one more breath
would ask too much
remember then

you come from here
there is no past that binds
no future that compels
no constraint upon this moment

it
is
all
all here

ED ROSENTHAL

The Digger

The lime vanilla ice-pop seen from a mile away
was a woman pushing a stick in the ground.
The wind romanced her rough robe
blowing cotton petals in and out
Her splotched white Dandelion of hair
flung itself around her arms and shoulders

Now half mile out the flimsy white head green cloth flapping
She was boat of bones flying a flag
pulling a wood anchor in a sand ocean.

The lips of the moon whispered--------
"Go to makeup ridge where earth grew
in giant mascara tubes."

My shadow climbed the hillside breathing heavy to the apex
where an effervescent coyote greeted me with a
muzzle tilt to the moon
A glowing cholla cactus discarding limbs in a pile alongside
grew an arbor of copper spines around us
from coyote's muzzle to his fluffy rear
and from his flank over my shoulders

Coyote gained a look of suburban flair
green pajamas of plant fiber covered his
haunches tinged red in the red sky.

Suddenly our prison was time warped
inundated in lilac cloud underthings
discarded by eighteenth century
female clouds dressing for storms.
Layer upon layer a moist violet petticoat
swished heavy aerosol lilac mist which thickened
to cotton candy consistency

We two in languid sleepiness
Crammed in a dreamy blanket
inside a luxury box
Six by Twenty by Ten feet
Ready for sale ground floor
South Coast Plaza Retail ridge
"Eco Designs by Chocolate Cholla
includes man and Coyote"

But our heavy box of limbs broke free
ripped the umbilical of cholla
and we tumbled over the road as she
watched her big box baby bounce.

I was a mute Victim of Coyote's
howls with my head shoved
against his as we landed high up
in an upholstered corner of cactus
as-if posed for brother's selfies
together.

Over the busy muzzle of the dog
howling in the dense lilac
from the corner of my eye
I scanned the Ancient traffic logs
on makeup ridge

A grim man rode a white horse
over the road in a flowing robe
of wine and gold
from his riding boots to his face
ending at his chin in a Fu man chu.
and above his head
a round hat of Animal skin.

Coyote woke me again
when the remote road glowed
in another day's light and a black horse
galloped by from the other side
A doppelganger in the wind.

MARY KAY RUMMEL

Burnt Dress

Even in old age I need you,
your voice a ululation
across a meadow tracked
by the capricious ash grey hare.

Your words sprout
from my heart like mallow.
You tell me to claim
the wildness I once wanted.
Your words, stones
I keep fingering.

Beauty walks this world aging everything —
each colonnade, leaf, sparrow,
lintel, scarf, water bird.
I am an angel in a burnt dress.
I call you now from the square,
stalls hung with yellow roses and handbags.
So much stone here,
A starfall of stained glass.

One egret in a field.
The loneliness
of angels without
even the body of a shadow.

My breath spread so thin
that nothing's left but bone
white emptiness, whisper of ruins.
Weaving, forever weaving
into and out of this world.

NOTE: First published in *The Lifeline Trembles*.

California Morning Song

Olive tree bent on the hill,
bathed in expectancy.
Lavender, and white stone.

Sea wind turns the world transparent.
Jade shell
Pink Perfection camellia
water-cuts in sand

mutate on the zigzag border
between wholeness and coming undone.

The horizon a gold line,
broken by tankers and tall ships,
between visible and unseen.

How loneliness ends
though you are far from home.

How a sailor becomes
the oceans she sails across.

NOTE: First published in *The Lifeline Trembles*.

SONYA SABANAC

In That Banat Land

Long ago, before I was even born
in the far away flat land of Banat
where wind scatters the dust
and rivers lazily flow

      my sorrow was conceived.

In that same land, my great-great-grandfather
grew grapevine and believed
no animosity was stronger
than a glass of good, old Banat Riesling
drank with the salute for good wishes.

      The bullet did not care what he believed in.

His son, Zhiva, "muzikant,"
was the first violin at weddings and village fairs.
When fertile Banat fields delivered,
his music would praise the Autumn
and override the echo of Hapsburg Monarchy's guns,
but a "dying beast" needed new blood.

      Zhiva played his last czardas on the Hungarian bomb

leaving my grandmother a pitiful
nickname that in whispers followed her
with its sad sound like a funeral march,
"posmrche" — a child
born after its father gone.
But that was not enough!

The second big war froze the Banat fields
one desolate night,

    my grandmother's second born had to go.

Different uniforms and languages,
marched the land of Banat.
For four years, a boy, who would
become my father, dreamt of a day
his father would come back home.

    In 1945 an unknown alcoholic man, claiming
    to be his father, came to stay.

Forty seven years later,
at the time of blood and betrayal,
I sought refuge in that land,
but I forgot what I should not have,
my grandmother's genes in me
would repeat her fate,

    my second born has passed away.

The pain made me run,
run so far away,
determined to break the curse of that flat land
I hid my first born in the New World,

    I let her cut the ties and become
    someone else.

NOTE: First published in *Grateful Conversations* anthology, 2018.

MARGARET SAINE

Interlude 1900

No more battle scenes
daubed in blood:
history painting
was finally dead

Only paintings of
landscapes, placid houses
people in Sunday reverie
fishing, drinking and talking
taking a walk
in the sunshine or
under green linden trees
in the half shade
and then May Cassatt's
lovely pensive women
holding their babies

Times were
no more pacific
but only paintings afforded
glimpses of peace

But then there were those
who muttered that Monet
bored them frightfully
with his hay heaps

And armed themselves
to the teeth
for the next war

Awakening

> *the forgeries of ourselves we were*
> *~ Laura Riding*

When intuition sleeps
it goes on the trip
of dreaming
drowning

A hushed penumbra
of darkened galaxies
in a flare of bright light
illuminating
the terminating flight

As intuition absorbs
wisdom from stars
to bring it back
onto the pillow
from the lips of night
to the threshold of day

The risen sun of intuition
wakes up and shines
in a display of phantom pain
over the loss of the night

SHAYMAA

Discovery

A shock of blue, the scrub jay
takes us down the trail to a
tree with pockmarked bark.
Each hole is an acorn home.
They glint like a child's hoard.

The hillside is a dark enigma,
the torrential river below
hushing its tell. Tree green
and shadow black cavort,
drawing passerby inquiry.

The fire licks at the darkness,
and rain whispers into the air. No
one sees the grey cinders burn
white hot as a raindrop here and
there soothe the fire to a smolder.

A shimmer of blue-grey and
the day is gone. Settling to sleep,
the breathing nearby is delicious
temptation. No one has a name,
a history. When in a dark room,
the known and the secret look the same.

Wild Life

The clouds are a stained glass ceiling,
a skylight. The trees everywhere are
fingers, dirty hair, broccoli for kings.

Pay attention. Inhale the surroundings
from the mountain top. How do people
enjoy nature when hiking?

Being slow, I notice a salamander
with steps like babies, like vulnerability.
I notice the tick who hungers for my blood,
the wind in a quiet circumambulation
of the Great Spirit.

The hills are a Gothic landscape, painted
by an auteur with only emerald, black,
and blue. The fog is a slowly reaching hand,
creeping toward trails that are moody footsteps.
I lead everyone, then fall behind, first finding the
trail, then letting it find me.

Getting lost here, starting a fire,
the darkness of everyone's faces,
subtle bundling, a sort of sudden
comfort from being in the same place
with strangers who smile and tell stories and
eat banana bread cookies without
seeing them in the dark.

PARAM SHARMA

Government Memorandum

1.
With reference to the above
I have the honor
To have been directed
To communicate to you
The interim decision of the Board
Pending the approval of the Commission
And subject to such said approval
Which is to say
That what has been said
And what is being said
As well as what will be said
Is to be construed as
Until and unless confirmed
By the aforementioned authority
With deletions additions and alterations
As the case may be
Provisional.

2.
Having regard to the nature
Of the discussion held
Over the request made
And taking into account
Your field of knowledge
Particularly
Your area of specialization
And considering
The degree of your involvement
Not ignoring
Your kind of experience

Nor
Your region of residence
I can say with certainty
That the likelihood
Of the possibility
Of giving effect to
The matter in question
Seems
In the present circumstances
Probable
In the near future
Perhaps.

3.
But in view of
The dire need for Health Educators
And the urgent necessity
To fill these needs
As soon as possible
And bearing in mind the foregoing
I have to say
That I am in a position
For the time being
To offer you
Tentatively and
Alternatively
The post of
Temporary
Supernumerary
Deputy
Assistant
Health Education Officer
Acting
In lieu of
The one under reference.

RICK SMITH

St. Germain District, Paris, 1949

My dad sets up his easel
in the ruins of St. Germain
and I get to amuse myself
in the post-war debris.
Concrete slabs and twisted rebar
throw mad shadow in the morning sun.
My dad takes a charcoal stick to the blank
canvas, roughs out
what's left of an apartment building.
Stained canvas becomes a battlefield
The hand and the stick depend on tension.
Six steps lead up to nothing,
fascinating to me or to someone
who studies destruction.
We try to imagine the noise this
would have made but the kids
went deaf
before they went blind,
went senseless before the skin peeled away
from the shock of fire.
Theory and speculation no longer matter. There
is disregard for the form and content debate.
There is no counting of ambiguities;
it all goes up in a flash and
it all goes up as one.

But this is about art,
illusion that sustains us.
Dad sketches out the one piece
that is still recognizable as wall
while I break rock and
darkness falls.

NOTE: Published in *Rattle* No. 16, Winter 2001.

KATHI STAFFORD

Near Belur Temple

> *The playful daughter of a Hillman is feeding jackfruit*
> *to a black-fingered monkey . . .* **Kapilar**

The girl can't stop herself. The monkey
keeps begging and she goes on handing
him treats, piece after piece.

Cardamom blankets
the evening scent. Incense
burns behind bushes.

She's anxious—knows her pet
will have a tummy ache,
but hands him jackfruit again,

Because the planets are beginning
to glow along the horizon. Soon clouds
will dip down their holy smells.

She pulls her turquoise sari
close around her skinny self.
The silk a present from the older sister,

the grave one who played the mother
but can always bring the child

Ripe Moon

In West Texas   a tan house with a dusty brown yard
Parents with a wounded baby listen to a mazurka
What would Chopin think of this mystery
Where we wet rags before the dust storm to stuff in windows
joy comes from small girls playing Peter Pan
While they joust in the heat   With red lips bloomed by
Hot cinnamon sticks from the candy store in the
Latina's front room   Where I learned to love sweets and
Spare change
Monet's wheat stacks rest on the wall a
Ripe moon casts shadows around the calm stubble
Increase our bounty O Lord   Increase our peace

JULIA STEIN

After the Fire Storm

We hiked into the burnt-black Simi hills,
headed past a forest of black shrubs,
saw tiny green buds beginning to grow,
stopped at the sandstone rock quarry where
the foundation stones of Los Angeles were dug,

climbed up footholds of the rock wall to the top
to see four leeching ponds cut into sandstone
where Chumash women leeched the acid out of acorns,
yes, we could learn from them how to cut into stone
and leach acid out of plants to get the hidden nourishment.

We walked up to the stone ruins of the stagecoach house,
saw blackened weeds in the middle of stone cisterns,
started hiking up the brown-stone devil's slide where
once a stagecoach route cut across the hills; now
we can learn to find the path through the stony land.

We saw against the black ash a green weed
with stinking yellow lemon gourds--the calabash.
Yes, we need to be green weeds and lemon gourds

stinking up the blackness of this city, saying we can
grow again, making this city a good green place.

MELISSA STUDDARD

Inside the beige brick house, the beige rooms

and beige-shirted people sit beautiful as unbuttered
biscuits, their awful loveliness upon me. They want me
drier than wheat and so still no marbles can roll
from my head. I want summer flashing the yard
red with begonias. I want Ladder-backed Woodpeckers
knocking at the gables, and Crepe Myrtle blossoms
blown down like hot pink cotton in a storm.
I'm embarrassing like that. A walking faux pas no one
wants to be seen with at the mall. I know love like
the arms of a cactus. I know the scent of earth revealing
her secrets after a much-needed rain. I buried
everything they told me to bury. Then, I dug it up again.

NOTE: Originally published in *Cutthroat: A Journal of the Arts.*

My Kind

My life's burning
That's what I mean when they ask how I am and I say
Fine. Rope-dangling, kicking-the-chair-out-from-under-me
fine; flirting-with-blades fine; looking-for-Pallas-Athena-
in-my-pancake fine (why would she visit that twerp Telemachus
and not me?) In my spare time, I'm building a death out of sad
songs and leftover,
microwavable food. I'm building a life out of
sad songs, good friends, and leftover microwavable food.

It occurs to me that I may be my own soul mate.
That's how I've ended up
in this body alone. But science says self is not so simple.
I'm a mosaic of viruses, bacteria, and, likely, other people.
All of us making decisions together. Group hug!

I am my own kind. I'll learn to play piano.
Like Hélène Grimaud,
I'll see blue rising from the notes. I'll see children
swinging in a park by the ocean.
The music will evoke everything. A meaningful life.
All of this inside a drop of dew. I'll be an amateur bird watcher,
a volunteer firefighter, a gourmet chef, a great
humanitarian. I'll plant a prize-winning garden,
grow a pot farm. My hair is on fire. I'm running
out of time. Maybe I'll learn to paint. Get
a cat or a dog. Something sweet
that likes to cuddle and craps outside the house. Something
feral and one step from wild. Something that,
when the moon jumps in the lake,
will jump in after, howling, in love with the lake,
in love with the moon, in love with itself and every other
disappearing thing.
My kind.

NOTE: Published by *Tinderbox Poetry Journal*.

KONRAD TADEMAR WILK

The Grace of a Great Dame

> ...*cichym pokątnym szelestem, którym ratowali ojczyznę od tylu lat.*
> ~ Juliusz Kaden-Bandrowski (1885-1944)

In amber was your mind conceived, your soul wrought
When the northern winds sang, your voice was born, your
words became the words my mother spoke, the words I sought
and when the first trees were born, your *szelest* was heard

Across the groves to the foundries where your blessed steel —
— was honed into the scalpel and the stylus sharp
A clear and clean sound hand plucked on a harp, to feel —
— the silent stirrings of Jarnsaxa's heart, unstressed —

— calmness to be found on a sunny day after rain
A full blossoming of *dziki bez, czarny*, sweet
and bitter like the journey through Oweynagat, pain —
— that meanders through your life, victory and defeat

I see you now, at the top of the stairs, a flame
You illuminate me, with grace of a great Dame

NOTES: On the 105th birthday of Dr. Alicja Burakowska née Dąbrowska, born 14 December 1913. She grew up in Warsaw and graduated from the Medical Academy before the start of World War II. In 1984, along with her husband, Polish Resistance fighter Marian Burakowski, she received the Medal of the Righteous Among the Nations from Yad Vashem, Israel, for saving 36 Jewish people during German occupation of Poland, 1939-1945. My maternal grandmother, and "second mother." She died in the city of Lodz, Poland on April 25, 1996.

In Polish: "...cichym pokątnym szelestem, którym ratowali ojczyznę od tylu lat"– *a quiet, hidden whisper with which they have been saving the homeland for so many years;* "dziki bez, czarny"– *wild lilac, black.* "Jarnsaxa"- a heroine from Norse myths. "Oweynagat" – a cave in Ireland, known as the Gate to Hell.

In Nonsymmetric, Entropic Gravitation

On Pierre de Fermat's 412nd (+/- 3) birthday

> That is not dead which can eternal lie.
> And with strange aeons even death may die.
> ~ *The Necronomicon*, H.P. Lovecraft

There is a wolf at the edge of the scalar field
Dreaming the Saturn year plucked bitterly in strings
Diffused conceptions that only the graced can wield
Look at the fang and the claw, the full moon has wings

Entropy guides the hand of the dreamer, valence —
— defines the motion of the leap of faith, I hate —
— to be manipulated, I live for the dance
and I don't take kindly to silly switch and bait

If the coffee tastes foul — it is the water that —
— matters and fools are like sheep for the wolves, set free —
— at the horizon of the point — particle, Fermat —
— laughs at you from his grave, as you hide the debris...

...which can eternal lie ... for the *maxima and*
— *minima* will be truth's adequality end.

AMBIKA TALWAR

Quantum of Your Gaze

How many layers of stories must be peeled away before we can find truth? And when we have found this truth, how do we know it for having lived with illusions for millennia? How then will we recognize truth of peace and of love that we seek? Will we know it when we come face to face with it? Is it the mirror into which I look daily?

Who are you? Stone, flower, petal, tender satin of desire, a mango, a fig, a date, a pomegranate. A molecule of light, sunrise, quantum of your gaze, breeze that makes music.

Who are you? I am strings of cosmos, song of the underbelly, Avatar, womb of cosmos – the great Mother Goddess...

Om bhur bhuvah svaha
Tat savitur vare niyam
Bhargo de vasya dhi mahi
Dhiyo yo naha pracho dyaat

NOTE: This excerpt first appeared in *My Greece: Mirrors & Metamorphoses*, 2016. In the mantra, Mother Gayatri is invoked for her blessings of ultimate illumination from the Sun in all aspects of life.

Love the Rain!

Pouring on our shoulders
rain washes away land, oceans, desires
Love the rain! You command
in a note on a burnt autumn morning.

What have you to wash away? What do I?

I love drenching my desires in silver rush –
remembering days when we ran freely on edge,
soaked toes squishing in naked puddles.
Laughing, we parted clouds to see gods peering.

Somewhere else floods push through doors.
Lone boney kitten shivers on broken wall;
hungry bread sinks sloppy helpless – uneaten.

Tender flowers topple in slim muddy grey world.

You used to fold paper boats, fit them
on shapely palms – race them curving
in puddle-slush – teeth so helplessly happy;
I wish we could walk in the rain again and again
cleanse away pain of living, of ceasing.

When drought seeps through layers
earth cracks between toes – nothing is promised;
pads of feet harden to crack as found leather.

Show me rainbows arcing over
our childhood boats, over your blinding eyes.
Message flutters on soil-fragrant windowsill
silver rush blurs the ink – words of love

>   make my fingertips smudge blue.
>   Am I drowning in thoughts of you?

JUDITH TERZI

Ode to Malala Yousafzai

She is a pool of gleam.
She is a seed, the rain.
She is a prairie of idea,
the harvest of motion.
She is rosewater
in a sandstone bowl.
She is the refugee, the tarp
of tent, the flame of fugue.
She is the arms of mothers,
a ribbon in a porcelain moon.
She is a lioness and loneliness,
the newborn swathed in pink.
She is earth yellow,
jade, aquamarine.
She is a threshold,
an arch, a minaret.
She is every headscarf--
magenta, amethyst, celeste.
She is our hands, our pen.
She is majestic, magnifique.
She is a luminous lagoon.
She is the sea--*il mare,*
la mer, el mar.
samandar.

NOTE: First appeared in *Malala: Poems for Malala Yousafzai* (FutureCycle Press, 2013).

Nostalgia

Like I'm waiting for kismet. *Maktoub*.
Waiting for a number, a letter--cryptic
for stage, grade. How many nodes
did she twist away? How many, how
many... Tell me to focus on healing.
Friends bring guavas, mini pumpkins,
t-shirts, pens, soup. The house
is a garden: five white orchids, purple
tulips, yellow roses, irises. Red
bromeliad clinging to bark, shape
of a seahorse, air plants cresting on two
heads. Rearrangement happening
in cachepots. Rearrangement of a colon,
color of geranium in a Casbah courtyard.
Animal on hooks in back rooms
of butcher shops where my grandfathers
blessed meat. How did she swing my
transverse meat around to greet my
small intestine, my distal ileum?
I wanted to catch the now-missing
slice as it slipped through her slick
incision above my navel. To feel
the surgeon's finesse navigate inside me,
caress my organs, then choke the cecum,
the appendix to death. How will the new
partners jibe? How will they groove
with no past in such diminished time?
No memory of all the little madeleines
and Sunday's flow of hours. Slippery
fingertips straining to hold onto a waltz.

NOTE: Finalist, *Solstice Literary Magazine*,
2019 Summer Contest Issue.

BORY THACH

In the Moonlit Night

Passing waves of crescent hills
Skulls of village warriors
Mound into pyramid temples
>> Thirty years—
>> The mute witness of the moon.

How to recall the god-kings,
Angkor among Tualang and dwarfed Strangler figs
Like a Barrier Reef—
>> Tower above
>> The surrounding water.

Churning moat of milk, the monkey-god
Of Ramayana, gestures from inside
The stone—
>> Fifty-four hand-carved mountains
>> Faces guarding points on a compass

Eyes half closed,
Smiling their irony
Not stinting their pity

Here in the moonlight.

Lost Tribe

Here the land is covered with nothing but dust throughout the year, until winter and the hope of rain hover above snow-capped mountains. At night I wonder if the unpaved roads lead back into town, or to Babylon, while I search through sandstorms in camouflage. My hands carry only a compass and map I haven't learned to read yet, only cold breath in front of me as I run. The midnight breeze supports a wren on its flight from one barrel cactus to another, standing like totem poles guarding the city. Was there ever a chosen people destined for emerald hills, milk and honey flowing like water from a cistern? Instead of drought, instead of the wind whipping the fields and darkening the sky for days. The rain clouds could turn this land bright yellow like sunflowers in March.

I run, and the desert awakens at each foot fall, quartz and feldspar underfoot recall luscious grasslands of the savannas which are now the directionless white sand dunes.

G. MURRAY THOMAS

"Your Kidney Just Arrived at Lax"

The doctor told me as I lay in pre-op prep.
I envisioned a special chartered flight,
an entire airplane filled with organs.

Hearts with little heart shaped carry-ons.
They always watch the inflight movie
and cry all the way through.

Livers splurging on one last drink;
they don't think they'll be allowed
where they're going.

The lungs eye the spot
where the oxygen masks drop.

Corneas stare out at the passing countryside;
they always get a window seat.

The spleens are always complaining
about security
about the length of the flight
about the lack of leg room
(although they have no legs).

The gall bladder always gets in line
before his row is called.
And there's my kidney,
no doubt reading a book to pass the time
something classic: As I Lay Dying,
or Great Expectations,
or The Stranger.

All of them wondering
about the journey ahead,
about their new home,
about their new life

NOTE: Published in *My Kidney Just Arrived*, 2011

MARY TORREGROSSA

The Promise of Snow

Banished to the cloakroom
for talking in class.
"Be still," I was told
as my eyes adjusted
to the dimness of the long
and narrow room,
coats hung in happenstance
on shiny black hooks
with fat rounded tips
curving upwards in prayer.

The door closed
on the silence within.
Sitting on a step stool,
hot cheeks in bony hands,
my elbows made dimples
on my knees.

The winter light of the afternoon
floated in from thick window panes
behind me, and yet, it did not light
the farthest corner where a tall
metal cabinet held paper, pencils
and heavy textbooks
neatly stacked behind locked doors.

I turned away from the
shadows lurking there
to stand on tiptoe
looking out on bare branches
and the gray sky
that promised snow.

My chin perched on crossed arms
I gazed toward the red brick tower
and its ledges of stone, where big
bells rang every Sunday –
where brave starlings lit
to look about –

and I see the city
spread far and wide,
a vast hilly landscape
of two-story tenements
and chimneys and evergreens
set among the bristling silhouettes
of brown barren trees.

My talons scratch the granite ledge,
my body lifts, drifts through the sky,
the sound of wings pumping, rushing
towards the cold horizon
and the rocky shore
of silver green waters below.

YUN WANG

Futurescape

Thunder of applause
followed by rain on the desert.
A single yellow flower
opens from a cactus palm.

A child sleeps.
Oars navigate an opal sea.

The Sun will die in five billion years.
Ten million spaceships will depart
from its white dwarf corpse.

A kiss sparks
beneath a canopy of cherry blossoms.
Electricity of one thousand faces
carved in breathing stone
rushes from Notre Dame.

Protons will decay.
The Universe will dissipate
back into a sea
of space-time foam.

Child, you are the guide
in my journey. I climb on
the boat of your laughter.

NOTE: Published in *The Book of Totality* (Salmon Poetry Press, 2015).

Spring

Blossoms fade in withered red and apricots are tiny
Swallows appear in the sky
Green water swirls around houses
Willow catkins peel off branches in the wind
Where at the sky's edge does fragrant grass not thrive

Behind the wall is a swing beyond the wall is a trail
Beyond the wall a traveler passes
Behind the wall a girl laughs
The laughter wanes and the sound dies away
The heart is undone by the heartless

NOTE: By Su Dong-Po (1036-1101 A.D.), translated by Yun Wang, *Dreaming of Fallen Blossoms: Tune Poems of Su Dong-Po*, White Pine Press, 2019

MARI WERNER

Joshua Trees

She doesn't like deserts
but she's come with me to Joshua Tree
for the photos and the flowers,
away from other people's secrets.

My sister is losing my daughter,
as I already have lost her.

The Joshua trees stand
with their quirky arms
reaching for rocks and stars.
On the broad plains they look
like some off-planet orchard.
She says they dance at night
when no one is looking.

I see them
dancing
solo
like a daughter
or together
like sisters.

We stop to get shots
of a full moon over the mountains
with the troupe of Joshua trees
turning blurred in the twilight.

From the third planet orbiting the yellow dwarf star 27,000 light-years from the center of the 97-billionth galaxy

Do you feel emotions the way we feel them?
Do you consider your planet beautiful?
Do you have children and love them?
Do you fight wars and kill each other?

No.
No you couldn't
do that could you?
War?

That would make you
as crazy as we are.
Are you?

Does life on your planet depend on
death like it does on ours?
Are some of you loving and some of you hateful
and most of you a confounding combination?

Do you sit (if you have bodies
that are structured for sitting)
and put words together
in whatever it is you use
for language (if you have language)
and form communications
that question your own identity?

Do you ponder the nature of the universe?
Any conclusions?

Measuring

How much fun would it actually be?

If there were a lid on the barrel
the fun level for the monkeys
could be expected to be at or below
zero, depending on the size of the barrel,
the number of monkeys,
and the amicability or lack thereof
in their relationships to one another.
If there were no lid on the barrel,
it would likely become a barrel of
no monkeys within a matter of seconds.

Subsequent fun levels would depend
on the environment in which
the lidless barrel was standing.
A jungle or playground might
afford considerable fun, but in a posh home,
monkey fun could soar, while human
fun rapidly dropped into negative territory.
A busy freeway would quickly result
in sub-zero fun levels for all concerned.

Other questions arise.
Whose idea was this?
Where did they get the monkeys?
Did they consult with the SPCA
or veterinary or zoological services?
What provisions, if any,
were made for care of the monkeys
after departure from the barrel?

In short, there are too many unanswered questions.
Minimally, a disclaimer might be appropriate:
No monkeys were harmed in the making of this simile.

KATH ABELA WILSON

Childhood Wisdom

Holding the knot of a hard, hot pretzel, all the mysteries seem clear. As we ferry across the bay, above, distant, the gulls spiral and turn. I see invisible labyrinths they draw with their wings.

> and here below
> I know the dark
> is filled
> with fast moving
> flying fish

> clear summer evening
> getting ready for
> the great ball
> Mt. Fuji
> puts on her red dress

NOTE: First published in *Ekphrastia Gone Wild*, 2013.

> like a painting
> a blue heron . . .
> my heart lifts
> like a brush
> full of sky

NOTE: First published in *Atlas Poetica* #20, 2015.

Now a Garden

reach deep into this garden
touch unseen roots
busy with memory
listen as I turn
the gold leaved doorknob of the past

yellow petaled branches creak
gold hinges of a treasure box
in this ground
where we slept with yesterday
and rise as rose sandstone to surface

know paths by touch are halls
carved contours of estates that were magnificence
rub our golden pollened hands
pluck the sectioned orange
of what went before

on our heads we hold
the red cracked globe of tomorrow
flowers flame to honor that unknown
where familiar groves know well the footsteps
and fragrant entrances of ancestors

what is given here are wishes
for this to stay
our time to go beyond
as the bee sprinkles
where it cannot tell

so we with our gifts and tribute
come to plead for all of our endurance
to this garden bright with vision
let no disturbance come our love
to climb the old tree like a vine

and drop nasturtiums into the old pool
contemplate the rings where time
from our unknown makes visible
hope a trellis here for now
where we are happy lost

and wander bloom
garden paths all drunk
with citrus and with iris
we are this garden for now is always
our temporary paradise

what grows

the rocks
are only a cover for the green
it grows within the risky inner core
covered by mirrors in the rain

the earth within rises like a dream
the scribbled underpinnings
what happened when the living roots sunk deep
the doors long closed and now and then the crack

of cloth pulled back wrinkles of the day's crust tangle
with the growing rocks that seem so still
the mouth is but a cave
opened by the dark

the dark ink stone the artist brushes
with all that seems
hidden and their shapes
the mountains of the mind are piled

percussive and in strings
of gold and green

MARIANO ZARO

Synapse

> Santiago Ramón y Cajal proposed that
> neurons are not continuous throughout the body.
> The word "synapse" was introduced in 1897 by
> Charles Sherrington.

Soon, my father says,
you will put two silver coins over my eyes.

*You are going to be out of the hospital
in a couple of days,* I lie.

Neurons are not all directly joined in a reticulum.

The nurse just left. *The oxygen saturation is low,* she told me.
My father plays with the bed sheets,
as if kneading the fabric, making a nest.

Why is the ceiling so far away? my father asks.

Information from other cells enters neurons
through dendritic tentacles and exits
via a gap at the end of long axons.

He lifts her right arm, the one not attached to the iv,
and picks up imaginary fruits.
Perhaps they are delicate eggs—partridge or quail.
He places them on his chest.

What are you doing, Father? I ask.
I am bringing this home, he says. *Nobody should be hungry.*

In a neuron, the axon ends.

Is everybody here? my father asks.
Don't forget to lock the door.

Days and weeks go by. My father sleeps long hours.
Fewer neurons willing to reach across the synapse void.

My father will die with his eyes open.
As if wanting to touch, to be touched.

NOTE. The following language was taken, with small variations, from the book *Nerve Endings* by Richard Rapport: "Neurons are not all directly joined in a reticulum. Information from other cells enters neurons through dendritic tentacles and exits via a gap at the end of long axons."

An earlier version of this poem has appeared in the magazine *Pratik*.

PART 2

POETS LAUREATE OF SUNLAND-TUJUNGA

John Steven McGroarty
> Poet Laureate of California, 1933-1944

Poets-Laureate of Sunland – Tujunga

1. Marlene Hitt, 1999-2001
2. Katerina Canyon, 2001-2004
3. Joe DeCenzo, 2004-2006
4. Ursula T. Gibson, 2006-2008
5. Damien Stednitz, 2008-2010
6. Maja Trochimczyk, 2010-2012
7. Dorothy Skiles, 2012-2014
8. Elsa Samkow-Frausto, 2014-2017
9. Pamela Shea, 2017-2020
10. Alice Pero, 2020-2021

Village Poets of Sunland-Tujunga

1. Marlene Hitt (to 2019)
2. Joe DeCenzo
3. Maja Trochimczyk
4. Dorothy Skiles
5. Elsa Samkow-Frausto (from 2014)
6. Pamela Shea (from 2017)
7. Alice Pero (from 2020)

JOHN STEVEN MCGROARTY (1862-1944)

Born near Wilkes-Barre in Foster Township, Luzerne County, Pa., on August 20, 1862, McGroarty attended the public schools and Harry Hillman Academy in Wilkes-Barre, Pa. After working as a teacher he served as a treasurer of Luzerne County, Pa., 1890-1893. He then studied law and was admitted to the bar in 1894, practicing in Wilkes-Barre. In 1896, McGroarty move to Montana and was employed in an executive position with the Anaconda Copper Mining Co. at Butte and Anaconda 1896-1901. In 1901, he moved to Los Angeles, California and worked as a journalist and writer. He was elected poet laureate of California by the State legislature in 1933 and served in this position until his death in 1944. He wrote numerous books and dramas, including the popular Mission Play staged annually at the San Gabriel Mission. McGroarty was elected as a Democrat to the Seventy-fourth and Seventy-fifth Congresses (January 3, 1935-January 3, 1939). He retired from politics in 1939 and lived in his Rancho Chupa Rosa in Tujunga, CA with his wife, until his death on August 7, 1944. The mansion and surrounding grounds were donated to the city of Los Angeles, and now serve as the home of the McGroarty Arts Center offering cultural programs, art and music classes to the local community. His most famous poem, "Just California" was often reprinted and recited on public occasions, copied in manuscripts, and even crocheted as a home decoration!

Just California

'Twixt the seas and deserts,
   'Twixt the wastes and waves,
Between the sands of buried lands
   And Ocean's coral caves,
It lies not East nor West,
   But like a scroll unfurled.
Where the hand of God hath hung it,
   Down the middle of the world.

It lies where God hath spread it,
   In the gladness of His eyes,
Like a flame of jeweled tapestry
   Beneath His shining skies;
With the green of woven meadows,
   And the hills in golden chains,
The light of leaping rivers,
   And the flash of poppied plains.

Days rise that gleam in glory,
   Days die with sunset's breeze,
While from Cathay that was of old
   Sail countless argosies; i'
Morns break again in splendor
   O'er the giant, new-born West,
But of all the lands God fashioned,
   'Tis this land is the best.

Sun and dews that kiss it,
   Balmy winds that blow,
The stars in clustered diadems
   Upon its peaks of snow;
The mighty mountains o'er it,
   Below, the white seas swirled —
Just California stretching down
   The middle of the world.

MARLENE HITT
First Poet Laureate of Sunland-Tujunga
1999-2001

The founding member of Village Poets, Marlene Hitt is a Los Angeles poet, writer and retired educator with local history as an avocation. She served for many years as Archivist, Museum Director and Historian at the Bolton Hall Museum in Tujunga. She is a native Californian and a graduate of Occidental College. As a member of the Chupa Rosa Writers of Sunland for nearly 30 years, she has worked with this small group of poets from whom has sprung readings at the local library, the Poet Laureate Program of Sunland-Tujunga, and the Village Poets. Ms. Hitt served a Poet Laureate of Sunland-Tujunga in 1999-2001. She has published a book on local history, *Sunland-Tujunga From Village to City* (Arcadia, 2000, 2005) based on columns written for the *Foothill Leader*, *Glendale News Press*, *North Valley Reporter*, *Sentinel*, and *Voice of the Village* since 1998. Her poems appeared in *Psychopoetica* (UK), *Chupa Rosa Diaries of the Chupa Rosa Writers*, Sunland (2001-2003), Glendale College's *Eclipse* anthologies, *Chopin With Cherries* (2010), *Meditations on Divine Names* (2012), *Sometimes in the Open*, a collection of verse by California Poets Laureate, and *The Coiled Serpent*, anthology of Los Angeles poets, edited by Luis Rodriguez (2016). She published chapbooks *Sad with Cinnamon, Mint Leaves,* and *Bent Grass* (all in 2001), *Riddle in the Rain* written with Dorothy Skiles, a stack of poetry booklets for friends and family, and most recently a critically acclaimed poetry volume, *Clocks and Water Drops* (Moonrise Press, 2015).

Arrival

Please, come home.
Walk into the door of the kitchen
where stew and wheaten bread
steam, where a fire warms.
Your father will tune the strings,
unwrap the bodhran.
I will uncover the harp.
The stew will simmer.
With hands wiped on my apron
I will open my arms
to you, my firstborn child
so long traveling. Your sisters
will dance. The old ones will smile
through brown, gapped teeth,
will smile blue into your eyes.
Wrapped around you, the old songs,
the scent of turf fire, the smell
of our own wool and you will sing.
While you sleep,
I will wrap around you a woven shawl
to shield you. Please come home
to bleating lambs,
to the resting place of love.

NOTE: First published in *Clocks and Water Drops* (2015)

Innocence

Once, the sky was a ceiling
with little holes
to let in the night air.
Once, the sky was a ceiling
to keep me safe between
earth and high places.
Once, the sky was a ceiling
with God on the other side
waiting for me to finish sleeping.

Now, in the blackness of night
standing on this lonely field
I look up and out.
The delicate hand of gravity
holds my feet, like mama's hands
holding my waist
while I leaned out too far.
My older eyes know
there is no safe ceiling
to catch the flyer. Never was
and if gravity lets me go
I will fly helplessly
out and out and out
into eternity, to forever.

Oh, how I wish
the sky was a ceiling
with little holes
to let in the night air.

Enlightenment

A dust devil blew in
from my childhood.
Dead leaves whirled up
from summer's hot soil
while a jay feather flew birdless
swirling into midsummer sky
up to the puffs of white cloud
as on the day when I was ten,
when I ran into the vortex
trying to find a secret
in the center of the whirlwind
only to rush away
with sand in my eye.
Why does that thrill return
as the wind whirls in?
And why, now, do I run away?

Prescription

A tincture could be made
of tears to heal,
anger turned to oil of wrath

then compassion, a balm
compounded on glass.

One drop tincture,
one drop oil
united with fragrant unguent.

The directions are clear:
touch lightly to bestow rest,
rub gently for relief.

Ancestors

> *Every layer they strip seems camped on before*
> Seamus Heaney

Whether the leather bonnets found in salt,
The fresh bones of ancestors beneath clean ice,
Meticulous stiches on the birch bark hat
Worn by a king, a rusted helmet
A linen blouse made of skin and fiber,
It doesn't matter. The life is gone.
A simple young woman, it is said,
Murdered for her transgressions
Was exhumed and examined, lifted
From a bog, her body looked into
By strangers, her story created
By invaders, her humiliation revived.

It is said
Another who was named Lucy
Once stumbled too close
To night-crusted tar
And now stands alone, through night and day,
Stared at.
Lucy from the tar.
The adulterous woman.
Warriors.
Kings,
Martyrs.
All are lifted out of the bogs, out of tar, from beneath glaciers
to become immortal.
If our warm bones hide in a safe place
Will we too inherit fame?
With a name not our own?

The Color of a Brisk and Leaping Day

You lean to a silver pond
in a brittle pose, staring
while circles try to reach you
the palette is dry
mudded to amber-brown

How unlike you
your stiff dropping
how unlikely on this silver day
for wind blew last night
to promise fair and sunny

I remember the amber
and the leaves deep gold
when the day itself leapt
far out into the colors
except red, which I banished.

That day you shook your hair
into the sand beneath the pond
and it came up gold.
That was the day we danced
into intersecting rainbows
each moment luminous and pure.

We twirled into the day
the one colored with laughter
that brisk and leaping
zestful soaring day
just the two of us.

Love Mended

That old threadbare word – love
flows in a fabric patterned
with shades of crimson colors,
whispers of mauve and the yellow of dry sun.
Chopin wove love into the air,
Monet stroked it onto canvas.

That word so often patched
nearly falls apart, its meaning frayed –
until a newborn cries
or a daughter becomes a bride,
until the lace of fifty years together
fully knits. Love unravels
until a friend perceives and cherishes,
until there is an ear ready to listen,
a shoulder to cry on. Love is repaired
with the consecration of all the threads.

Then, there is delight in love's stitching,
the worn word renewed
into the One Love.
Mended.

NOTE: Written upon request from the Rotary Club of Sunland-Tujunga
and first published in *Clocks and Water Drops* (2015).

The Remembering

She says she remembers
the dark meat of grouse
chunky with bites of buckshot,
cabbage fried in bacon grease,
one pot of potatoes for eleven children.

He says he remembers
sugared tomatoes stewed in the warm kitchen,
flour-and-milk pudding on a snowy day
with brown sugar and nutmeg.
The days they salted the pork.

She remembers
the root cellar full of salamanders,
chickens and peas and jams in jars,
muddy prints on the scrubbed floor,
hot water on the side of the stove.

He remembers
digging the well. Twilight harvests.
Piling manure on the side of the house,
ferrets in the henhouse,
the cow that nearly gored his mother.

She remembers
the one tin dipper in the wooden water bucket,
the babies coming one after the other,
the grandmother, the hired hands,
Sunday dinners, so many pies.

He says he remembers
the day they brought the Rumley home,
the joy of an easier days' work,

the calving, the horse with colic,
the Northern Lights.

She says she remembers the story
of her father coming home
over unmarked prairie,
the horses leading through blizzard,
the dot of lamplight in the frosted window.

He remembers the story
of the day a mother loaned blankets
to fevered, trail-weary men.
In a month children died,
throats closed, breath trapped inside.

She remembers
her first sight of the city
the day after they eloped,
the room they stayed in,
the frame garage that became their home.

He remembers
the job that took him from her,
the full, sweet moments of coming home,
their small corner drug store,
built together. The children.

They say they remember
as they hold hands,
speak about the new ways of things,
and of their old world
which has passed away.

NOTE: First published in *Clocks and Water Drops* (2015)

KATERINA CANYON
Second Poet Laureate of Sunland Tujunga
2001-2004

Katerina Canyon is a 2020 Pushcart Prize Nominee. Her stories have been published in *New York Times* and *Huffington Post*. From 2000 to 2003, she served as the Poet Laureate of Sunland-Tujunga. During that time, she started a poetry festival called "Shouting Coyote Poetry Festival" and ran several poetry readings.

She was featured in the *Los Angeles Times* and was awarded the Montesi Award from Saint Louis University in 2011, 2012, and 2013. She has published multiple chapbooks and an album. Her recent books include *Changing the Lines*, a volume of poetry, and *Los Angeles Nomad*, a novel. You can find more information about her on her website, poetickat.com.

Feet

I cleaned my daughter's feet.
I swept the warm cloth along
her soft, Earth toned skin - she grinned
and said, "Mom, that feels Heavenly."

Yes, I remember.

Lying on the bed like a doll filled with sand
too fatigued to move - I played hard that day.
Slightly waking to feel the warm cloth on my feet.
Mother washing the day's dirt away.
Yes, that felt Heavenly.

My friends told me their mothers would say
we should always take care
to wear clean underwear
in case we came upon disaster.
"Clean feet are most important", my mother said.
She explained that a woman's feet
told the story of her life.
That on her soles you could see
the roads she traveled.
She would say, "You can measure her resilience
in a woman's ankles"
I was told that if I were to get into an accident,
dressed like a bum,
and the doctors saw I had clean feet,
they would take good care of me.
"I know that may sound silly to you"", she'd say
She explained they would know that I tried
my best to take care of myself
and that my dress was more
a matter of circumstance than of desire.
When I was too tired for an evening bath, she washed my feet.

When I was sick in bed, she washed my feet.
When we were homeless, she washed my feet.
When she felt there was nothing else to do,
she washed my feet.

Yes, it felt Heavenly.
I tried out for the high school track team.
I went in for a physical.
The doctor examined my feet
and said, "Nice feet," and approved me as healthy.
He never asked me if I had on clean underwear.
I wondered how many kids
would miss out on running track
because their feet weren't as clean as mine?
And I thought she was being silly.
She was right.
I finally saw her.
And there she was.
Too tired to move.
Dying.
I filled the bowl with warm water.
I found a soft cloth.
Picked up the soap. Ivory pure.
The only type she would use.
I looked at her feet - so long and thin.
Dark as Louisiana clay.
Her veins stuck up like river lines.
A road map to the Bayou.
I washed her feet.
Her feet carried heavy burdens.
She walked many miles for many years.
She said, "That feels Heavenly."

I replied, "Yes, I remember."

Why write?

Gil Scott Heron stands on the corner
of talent and reverence with a battered
and dingy sign
that reads
will work for Crack

That's his inspiration
and even so
his words are infrequent
due to the greater
love of drug than verse

Yet his lyrics still skitter
along his music
like an electrified flea
dancing to the infused hum
of verse and tune

Inspiration and words come
and go and once released

Escape into the fog of the butane

smoke

It leads to the search
for more time
and no explanation
for words

Where there
are no reasons
for words
you look to the high

from crack

from food

from sex

from violence

from pain

to give you a feeling
a reason
a meaning
an excuse

For the words

The Color of Their Skin is What Defines Most People, so Barren

But you and I are completely exquisite,
you said, as most do when minds combine.

When you and I first met, no, nix that,
it was a little later,
in the woods, and you took me to
see the crisp snow, in the Cuyamaca
Mountains, when the first flake kissed my lips.

That is when I first saw color.

      "O"

          As hollow as the sound.
          An infinite wall
          protecting emptiness.

Material Value

I
I
I
I am a woman

I am a woman

I am not the spoils of war

I am not an instrument for barter
I am not the reward for victory

I do not come with a price tag.

This
This
This
This is not how you value me

You do not take me
You do not rape me
You do not turn my children into soldiers

I am the mother of thousand generations
I am the daughter of a million ancestors
I am the sister of humanity

My face does not launch a thousand ships
My eyes are not to die for
My body is completely resistible

I
I
I
I am a woman

Penance

I am memories
        wrapped in dark skin

absorbed by tissue and bone.

The notes I take serve as branded
relics of my tribulations.

Like a mural painted on quicksand
the mind cannot
        fix recollection.

When there is no palette with oils to mix,

When God recalls
        the art I choose to display without praise,

the whip's lash as steel-brushed strokes
across wrought iron flesh from fire,

learned from my parents,
in turn from their mammas and daddies,
handed down from the plantation,

what will I say?

This is my art.
        Inspired by God's flood.
                          His pestilence.

The bruises were his marks upon Cain
        the blood - the pain - upon Eve.

I will not ask forgiveness for denying him,

Just as He will not ask for mine.

A Cento for Poe

The angels, not half so happy in heaven
Because I feel that, in the heavens above,
At morn-at noon-at twilight dim-
To friends above, from fiends below,
the indignant ghost is riven.

Eternal dews come down in drops
By a route obscure and lonely,
With storms -- but where meanwhile
Joy's voice so peacefully departed
murmuring in melody.

So shake the very Heaven on high
O God! on my funeral mind.
I mourn not that the desolate are
happier sweet, than I
But to be overcast, a voice from the future cries.

An angel throng, bewinged, bedight
In veils and drowned in tears,
Comes down -- still down -- and down
Where the good and the bad and the worst and the best
Can struggle to its destin'd eminence.

JOE DECENZO
Third Poet Laureate of Sunland Tujunga
2004-2006

JOE DECENZO grew up in Los Angeles and majored in theater and English Literature. From 2004-06 he served as the poet laureate of Sunland-Tujunga. He produced the "Shouting Coyote" Performing Arts Festival and was a Department of Cultural Affairs grant recipient. His published works include *The Ballad of Alley and Hawk* and the *Study Guide and Poetry Primer* for the same collection. His poetry appeared also in *Meditations on Divine Names* anthology (Moonrise Press, 2012). He currently serves on the planning committee for the Village Poets of Sunland-Tujunga, as Chair of the Poet Laureate Search Committee, and as Chair of the Arts and Recreation Committee of the Sunland-Tujunga Neighborhood Council.

Ordinary Rose

In a less than perfect world
With inadequate direction
There are numerous reminders
Of astonishing perfection.

They appear in many forms
Some still hidden, I suppose
And the greatest indication
Is the ordinary rose;

Every petal purely placed
To form an iridescent glow
Around a stamen soft and sweet
That bears the scent all lovers know.

And I want my art to flourish
In this manner I propose
And I dare as much to ask,
How do I create a rose?

Conversing with the Shadows

She revels in conversation of the big bands
that once accompanied her in nightclubs and lounges
around Hollywood during its time of glory.
She remembers the songs but not the words.
She remembers the bandleaders but not their names.
She thinks it was a hat but can't remember "Brown Derby."
She knows she was a singer, but can't remember Ciro's.
She can't remember checking coats
or selling gum and cigarettes from a wooden tray,
but she remembers she was great!

She once danced with Van Johnson, sang next to Bing Crosby,
was mentioned by Luella Parsons and
romantically linked to Victor Young.
She even told a flunky for Howard Hughes to go screw himself
when he told her Mr. Hughes desired her company.

The 78's spun round and round;
heavy black shellac that held the record of her voice.
The fragile paper labels with her name and titles printed
reminding her "I'm In The Mood For Love,"
"My Foolish Heart," and "I Only Have Eyes For You"
spun as wildly and dizzily as the lifestyle she lived.
Her days started and noon and rarely finished before 3:00 am.

It was the golden age of her life and creativity;
the basis of the stories she would tell anyone interested in
hearing or hapless enough to be cornered in conversation.
It was the time she remembered; when the puzzle pieces fit;
when the loops and sockets, tabs and slots fit seamlessly
together, revealing images more splendid, more dazzling
than the cover of the box.

But it's 5 o'clock now, and twilight's focus fades.
She's sundowning.
Figments and fiction start dancing in her head
like the chorus at the Macambo.
The glimmer in her eyes drifts to a vacant hallow stare.
She staggers to her dresser and dons three brassieres.
Fragile as a teacup balanced on a knitting needle
she teeters at the couch because she's not sure where to go.

She thinks she knows you. She must.
You're in the same room.
She simply addresses you with "Hey gorgeous,"
"How are ya' love," or "What's cookin, honey?"
because a name won't come to mind.
She tells me how handsome I would be in a tie.
"Everyone wears ties where I go," she says.

She's angry at her mother, wants to see her father;
looks for her father.
"Dad, DAD!" she cries and franticly tears at the locks
of the front door to make her way outside to find her father.
Clarity is gone; nothing lucid left today.
She's talking with shadows and smoldering memories
now locked in a soot-coated furnace
whose passion has no vent.

Barely Dressed

I'm covered in the dust of stones I've sculpted
Of roads I've paved and fires I've provoked

I'm swaddled in the haze of fantasies I've woven
Of stories I've concocted and burlap hopes that do not fit

I invent the things I've yet to see, devise the tools I can not hold
And contrive mercy for things I do not feel

The grass is damp and stains my pants
But lets me drift between memory and narcotic sleep

So let me dream for air is scarce
I gasp for breath while choking on the fiction I inhale

I search for pearls in a clam and dig for water in the desert
While vainly trying to hang wall paper in a windstorm

I stand naked before those I can't accept
Scan the crowd to find a common voice

Flowers

I brought flowers that day
Because I thought they might dry her eyes
I brought flowers that day
Because my feeble tongue couldn't find the words
To make her smile
Not that day
I brought flowers that day
Because the ornaments and garland just weren't bright enough
And the foil tinsel, mockingly hanging,
Like the edges of a thousand knives cutting at her heart
Bore no sense of holiday
Not that day

Hoping that the petals would block her view
When she drew them toward her face
Or maybe just lend a dusting of color to her graying cheeks
But had I been thinking, I'd have brought a basket
To catch the heart that was falling from her chest.

I brought flowers that day because nothing added up
Everything was out of order and bass-ackwards
Like winter after spring or darkness after sunrise
To have a child precede a parent just doesn't make sense

I brought flowers that day because God was MIA
Or just too damn busy to see what he was doing
To the saintliest woman He ever created

And as for you, Reaper, you pathetic coward
Skulking in the early morning when you knew
I wouldn't be there to hold you back
Had I been there that day
I'd have put my boot so far up your robe
You could have flossed with the laces

I brought flowers that day
Because the attendant hurried us from the morgue
When he saw the tag that read "communicable"
And refused to let her see
I brought them because I felt useless and powerless
And it's harder to be angry
When you're holding flowers

My Companion in Free Fall

A poem hit my chin when I stepped through the cabin door
It ran down my neck like watermelon juice in July
It was both wet like rain and stingingly cold like snow
It was comforting the way it burned my skin
   and made me feel alive

It was uninvited yet welcome to light on my face
Like a bee trying to pollinate a flower
Surprising was its visit in that it wasn't the first day of spring
Or the last day of summer or any one of a number of holidays
   that might herald its arrival

It wasn't my anniversary nor the birth of my child
No kings were holding court, there were no victories to proclaim
There were no blooming meadows, no social issues to redress
God was not unkind, nor had my favorite singer died

Still, it stuck to me, this poem of mine
In the place where saliva collects when I am ravenous
In the place where words fall when they are aimlessly chewed
I let loose the cabin door and began my decent
The speed increased 32 feet per second squared
Until I was going so fast I felt weightless
Unaware of the clothes on my body or even
   the blood in my veins

In a minute's time, the ground began to quickly surge
Impact with the earth was certain
I pulled the poem my chin and screamed it toward the sky
It unfolded in a cascade of silk and nylon
Gathering all the air around
Suspending me on a beam of light
Until I wafted gently down

How fortunate was its arrival
On that uneventful day

For a Friend

I won't say goodbye, dear friend, just, I'll see you later.
I'll see you in the crested swells
And rippled sails at the marina;
On the wind carved hillsides
That coax me onto trails unexplored.
I'll see you in the mirage of rising heat from the highway
Of every road trip ventured
As you draw me toward unfamiliar places
And ignite my flames of joy.

It's a time for meditation, but not to say goodbye;
A time to say out loud
What I'd always hoped was understood;
A chance to clear the ledger
Of some long outstanding debt;
To pay you for your kindness
With the endless tears I wept;

To express in some small way
Your generosity survives
The desire and ambition
That surrounded both our lives;
To quietly recount the dreams
That never will come true;
A time for deep reflection
Of the immeasurable you.

DAMIEN STEDNITZ
Fourth Poet Laureate of Sunland-Tujunga
2006-2008

Marlene HItt, Ursula T. Gibson, Damien Stednitz, Katerina Canyon, Joe DeCenzo at the induction of Damien Stednitz as Poet Laureate, 2008.

Damien Stednitz's work has been published in *Speechless Magazine, Astropoetica, The San Gabriel Valley Quarterly, True Poet Magazine, Flintlock, Falling Star Magazine* and *Poetry Superhighway*. Additionally his poems appeared in various anthologies including *Looking Out of Pasadena* and *Sometimes in the Open*. He has authored three books, including *The Carter Variations* (2008). Stednitz has been a featured reader at various venues throughout Los Angeles and the central coast. During his tenure as Poet Laureate Stednitz organized a poetry reading during the Sunland Watermelon festival to bring poetry to the community at large. Top poets from the Los Angeles area participated. Stednitz participated in the annual 4th July parade in Sunland, sponsoring a float which increased awareness of the poet laureate program to the community. During the parade Stednitz performed readings and handed out over 50 CD's containing spoken word poetry and e-books. Stednitz was also a featured reader at various local events ranging from readings at McGroarty Arts Center to a local AARP chapter meeting at Sizzler.

Sunland

I live in Sunland, CA
It's off the 210
Sunland does not have a Home Depot
(it's a long story)
We do have a place where you can get
52 different types of burritos,
But it's kind of misleading because
They count a tortilla with just cheese
As one, and a tortilla with just cheese
And tomatoes as two, etc. etc.
They basically have 5 types of burritos
With roughly 10 ingredients, but still, they're good burritos

I was eating one of the 52 burritos
(beef, cheese, sour cream, and lettuce)
When I first heard about the Watermelon Festival
I had only lived in Sunland about six months and didn't realize
This was THE event of the summer
Bands, booths, funnel cakes, free watermelon
And a watermelon eating contest, what was there not to love?

Jayme and I went to the Watermelon Festival that weekend
It was almost mid-western in its charm
Toddlers ran around laughing, holding wedges of watermelon
As big as their heads
A country western band played
For me, being a recent arrival from the Midwest, I reveled in the
Simplicity ... the joy of cold watermelon on a smog free day
Eating watermelon in a watermelon eating contest
Is something you should do at least once before you die
I lined up with my five other competitors, the judge said go and
I buried my face in watermelon, chewing furiously, my eyes
Burned from the juice, my goatee an absolute mess, Jayme
Laughed I came up for air, chewing, gulping, hair matted,

T-shirt turning pink and then I noticed the guy at my complex
That always gets the mail the same time I do, he was cheering
For me, and the lady that works at the dry cleaners She cheered,
And the guy that cuts my hair was clapping and laughing, and
The lady from the water store smiled and pumped her fist,
They cheered for the new kid from Nebraska, I smiled a sloppy
Smile, and dived in and ate even faster

I got 2nd, in my heat, a Marine who I'm pretty sure
was part vacuum won the whole thing it was okay though,
I lost out on a medal, but I gained a community

This Smaller Murder

Kevin tells me that a group of crows is called a murder
Herd of cows, flock of seagulls, murder of crows
This is the kind of stuff that Kevin knows, random facts
Sputtered out like hot oil in a broken engine

Kevin and I shared a baby sitter as children,
I liked him then, he made me laugh, I still like him now
His thick glasses, constant smile, sporadic verbal gunfire
Kevin's simple delights in birds or ice cream or the wind

Three crows that live in the tree outside my bedroom window
Remind me often of Kevin, make me call him on Saturdays
When I don't want to but when I know I should
On our calls he talks of crows, (his favorite birds since Dumbo)
Or how the cornfields look when the wind hits them or his love
of go-carts or how I am his friend,
He reminds me of this often on our calls I guarantee Kevin
Frequently that I will always be his friend

Kevin's mom dies unexpectedly, asleep at the wheel
She works two jobs so Kevin can live at home
The family tree his mom and him live in .. .lived in, was a very
small tree Kevin and his mom occupied the sole branch

A Sarpy County sheriff tells Kevin's nurse, she tells Kevin,
she calls me - my crows sit on the branch outside the window
as I talk to Kevin, This would be hard for anyone
It's impossible for him, he cries, I tell him I'm his friend

Two weeks later I've already talked to the social workers
and the county. Now I talk to Kevin and I explain to Kevin
Why he can't come live with me in Los Angeles
The crows stare at me intently as I saw off Kevin's last branch
And guarantee him life in a cage
I assure him I'll call him after he gets settled in at Oakdale

As the phone hits the cradle, my three crows take flight
I watch them fade into the sky
I am haunted by this smaller murder

Details

I'm good at talking to people
I remember little things
I know when to keep talking, when to turn back
I smile and remember birthdays, kids' names, vacation spots
the details that breed trust
I coach people how to talk to doctors for a living
I remember the little things
I'm good at talking to people

the old woman in the waiting room forgets her husband's name
she has sliced tennis balls on her walker, her hands shake
her glazed eyes turn to me, turn back to her husband
Lauren and I smile politely and then continue
going over the pending detail
I coach Lauren how to talk to doctors for a living
I remember little things
the old woman in the waiting room forgets

the little girl is glowing, blonde curls
I watch the old woman's eyes follow the young light
she whispers "that girl makes me want for to turn back. .. "
her hand reaches weakly, brushes gold hair for a moment,
 a smile then Alzheimer's erases the details, her light dims again
Her husband coaxes her hand to her lap;
this is the life he's living
I remember little things
the little girl glowing, blonde curls

what good am I talking to people?
I want words for the old woman and her husband
words to turn it all back for them

words that say something that delivers a smile
words that remind them of the details of their past
but her light is going dim, erasing, he holds her hand, living
the little girl is glowing, blonde curls
the old woman in the waiting room forgets
and I remember these little things

The Carter Variations

my son is two weeks old
he is starting to see colors for the first time
he knows to eat and sleep
he has no dreams or aspirations or fears
his life at the moment is defined
by its sheer simplicity

at predawn
holding him, my mind takes me
through the Carter variations
the myriad of possibilities
the varied versions of my son
or possible sons

Carter, the young man who plays
bass guitar with rhythmic fluidity
and loves U2 and Van Morrison

Carter, the moppy haired boy
who at age five dresses as Calvin
to my Hobbes for Halloween

Carter, the doctor who marries
Katherine Jennings after Med School
and moves to Oklahoma City

Carter, who gets lost at the mall
and puts me through 48 minutes of hell
until I find him at security eating a Sno Cone

I rifle through these variations on a theme
as my wife sleeps and Carter coos in my arms
there are illness and people in this world
that would do him harm

but more importantly there are people
some I know, but many I have not yet met
that will be his greatest friends, mentors, allies and lovers

I hold in my arms not just my son, but my hope,
fears and dreams this six-pound boy is heavy with possibility
filled with blossoming complexities
I see an entire reality in his eyes
I am humbled and made small by the sheer
breadth of his future

To the Daughter I Didn't Have

I dreamt about you a lot
over the last five months
your name was Harper
and you had gold curly hair
and your mother's eyes
you laughed a lot and loved
Hello Kitty and sometimes
pulled our real cat's tail
but we allowed it because he's
de-clawed and your laugh made
it all worth it
your mom loved to dress you
in hats and dresses and bows
and there was a stack of comic books
that I had prepared for you in case you
were a boy that got forgotten under
dolls, and flowers, and a tidal wave of pink
(Your mom and I are educated enough to know
we shouldn't gender code but we did anyway)
and Harper it was going to be great
 a pink nursery with frills and ribbons
your mom and I had cleaned out Baby's R Us
of both their sugar
and their spice
I was ready for you in these dreams
to protect you from the world
my little girl
to save you from all the stupid boys
them of puppy dog tail origins
I would spin you on the merry go round
faster and faster, the wind filled with laughter
you convinced no one in the world

could be stronger or faster than
dad

Harper, you were vanished in a sonic boom
we saw that you were not the person we thought you were
on that grainy, lo-res screen
my dreams had misled me
Your mom giggled and somewhere a snake bought a snail a beer
the comic book stack grows daily
now I find myself wondering where I can buy a baseball glove
and Spider-Man has regulated Hello Kitty to the garage
where she waits for you, forgotten,
next to unopened bows & ribbons
autumn has come and in spring a blue hurricane will hit
Your mom and I enjoy the falling leaves,
the calm before the storm

I pushed a merry-go-round today, just once
while walking the dog, watched it spin
I heard a dream girl laugh in the wind

Harper I truly hope to see you again

URSULA T. GIBSON
Fifth Poet Laureate of Sunland-Tujunga
2008-2010

URSULA T. GIBSON, born in Germany in 1930, came to the USA in 1934). She served as the Poetry Editor for *Poetic Voices* from 1997 until 2005, at which time the on-line poetry journal ceased publication. On March 19, 2006, Ursula was installed as Poet Laureate for Sunland-Tujunga, California, for the two-year period. Her book, *The Blossoms of the Night-Blooming Cereus* (2005), was selected as First Prize winner in Poetry in the DIY Book Festival 2005 Competition. She has published three chapbooks (*Eyes*, 1990, *Two Tujunga Poets*, 1993, and *Spirited*, 1996), and *Be Prepared, Don't Mumble, Look UP! or How to Read Poetry Aloud* in 2003, a manual on oral interpretation). She was a member of California Federation of Chaparral Poets, Inc., (State Treasurer from 1997-2005) and of California State Poetry Society. She has been a legal secretary since 1956, and a California Certified Legal Secretary since 1989 when the four-hour exam first was given in California. Ursula was married for over 40 years to James B. Gibson, a professional astronomer, and lived in Tujunga, California. She died on December 9, 2013.

The Summer Has Fled

I opened the front door
and let Autumn wander in,
its cooler air and lesser sun
a relief from hot Summer.
We'd played and traveled,
we'd read books and made music.
We'd seen other houses and
met many people, but now
the Autumn was here,
and peace descended.

Preparation for cold weather,
making sure the animals were safe,
harvesting the hard summer work,
all awaited the first snow fall.

The trees dropped their leaves
and went to sleep for the winter.
We knew they would recover
when Spring returned.

The bare branches made us sad,
but we got out the winter clothing,
and waited for the snow to play in.
Winter would come and go.

And then it would be Spring again!
We would tend the flowers, mow the grass,
care for the animals, and enjoy riding,
and hope for good Summer to last forever.

Twelve

He stood so tall;
he was so kind.
When I was eleven,
twelve was on my mind.

One day, I said,
I'm going to miss you.
'Cause we're going away.
He said, "I want to kiss you!

Now, don't get angry at what I say.
You're my best friend, going away!"
I turned my cheek,
and my knees felt weak.

But twelve held my arms
and his eyes filled with smile.
As he kissed my mouth
my heart leaped a mile.

I think of twelve
though we've long been apart.
That velvet softness
Stole a hunk of my heart.

Driftwood Heart

I've walked along the beach,
picking up scraps of driftwood
for house decorations.
I think of you because
the pulse of waves up the sand
is your rhythm.

My heart is driftwood, too,
since you left me on the shore of life,
graying and bleached by sun.
The steady heat of waves of work
cover up the fragile driftwood heart
that can't find rest
on the labyrinth shore.

NOTE: First published in *Poetic Diversity*, 2006.

Improvements

Torn ground rips from the hillside,
bulldozers carving away ridges and
massive trucks departing with the earth!
Heavy machinery rumbles
to make a platform, terraces, trenches,
foundations; water pipes and sewer lines inlaid;
structure and framework, electricity, plumbing,
roofs, walls, doors and windows
for another hundred Californians to own.

But in the rain, the hillside bleeds
muddy rivulets of erosion, decay,
without wild oats, poppies, or golden mustard,
with live oaks destroyed and mesquite mangled,
monkshood wasted, primroses unblooming.
No coyotes singing or rabbits shyly hopping,
no ground squirrels or rattlesnakes,
no occasional opossum picking its way through brush.
No more blazing butterflies or scrub blue jays,
mockingbirds or red-tailed hawks soaring high,
and grimly, the candelabra yuccas succumb.
All nature raped for man's convenience and profit.

If we build over all of California's wild places,
why would anyone want to live here?

NOTE: First published in *Poetic Diversity*, 2004.

The Blossoms of the Night-Blooming Cereus

In weeks, the pimple of green on the side of the stem
grows outward, bends as the blossom head expands,
encased in its brachts, swelling day by day,
'til the tip whitens, the growth attains its goal.

That evening, the blossom unfurls, pressing sepals down,
revealing slender petals of cream
and pistils like fairy's hair,
a bold stamen asserting its power in the middle of them.
In two short hours, the blossom reaches its fullest extent,
eight inches wide of loveliness, exquisite in the darkness
against the tall greenery, awaiting the moth to fertilize.

It blooms all night, this creamy creation,
but in dawn's first light,
the flower folds and fades,
the brachts close over it again.
In two short days, the flower that was
is necrotic, black, and falls.
Left behind is a nub that may become fruit.
It depends on the success of the insects.

I am not like the night-blooming cereus.
I cannot force my energy and love
into one magnificent display.
My blooming takes years, and
my fruiting takes decades,
and my life lasts many nights
in which no response to my being occurs.

I may need to wait for an inner light
or an outer force
before I can reach fruition,

but I will grow and will open my petals
of mind and heart
and will expose myself to possible rejection
or being overlooked,

because staying closed up, unblooming,
defeats the purpose of life,
would make me wither before I've lived,
like the night-blooming cereus.

> NOTE: First published in *The Blossoms
> of the Night-Blooming Cereus*, 2005.

Time for Rest

The Evening strolled into the garden,
scattering shadows where the Sun
had left its patches of light,
and trees murmured in the Evening's breeze
to comment on the coming night.
The Evening provided a mood of caring
as it wandered on its way
to other gardens in the neighborhood.
The flowers closed their petals.
The time for rest was good.

> NOTE: First published in *Magnapoets*, 2009.

MAJA TROCHIMCZYK
Sixth Poet Laureate of Sunland-Tujunga
2010-2012

MAJA TROCHIMCZYK, Ph.D., is a Polish American poet, music historian, and photographer. She published seven books of poetry: *Miriam's Iris* (2008), *Rose Always – A Love Story* (2008, rev. 2020), *Slicing the Bread* (2014), *The Rainy Bread* (2016), *Into Light* (2016), and three anthologies, *Chopin with Cherries* (2010), *Meditations on Divine Names* (2012), and *Grateful Conversations* (2018). Her poems appeared in: *California Quarterly, Cosmopolitan Review, Ekphrasis Journal, Epiphany Magazine, Lily Literary Review, Loch Raven Review, Lummox Journal, Quill and Parchment, Pirene's Fountain, Pisarze.pl, Poezja Dzisiaj, The Scream Online, Spectrum* and anthologies by Poets on Site, Southern California Haiku Study Group, and others. As a Polish music historian, she published seven books, most recently *Górecki in Context: Essays on Music* (2017). She is the founder of Moonrise Press, President of Helena Modjeska Art and Culture Club, and President of the California State Poetry Society. Her research studies, articles and book chapters appeared in English, Polish, and in translations in ten countries. She read papers at over 90 international conferences and is a recipient of honors and awards from Polish, Canadian, and American institutions, such as American Council of Learned Societies, the Polish Ministry of Culture, PAHA, McGill University, and the University of Southern California.

What I Love in Sunland

1.
The strong arms of the mountains
embracing, protecting our town

2.
The lights scattered in the night valley
during my drive to the safety of home

3.
How clouds sit on the hilltops
squishing them with their fat bottoms

4.
The river playing hide-and-go-seek under the bridge
to nowhere: "now you see me – now you don't"

5.
The towering white glory of yucca flowers in June –
we are Lilliputians in the giants' country

6.
The mockingbird's melodies floating above
red-roofed houses asleep on little sunny streets

7.
Armenian fruit tarts sweeter than fresh grapefruit
and pomegranate from my trees

8.
Hot, shimmering air, scented with sage and star jasmine,
carved by the hummingbird's wings

9.
The rainbow of roses, always blooming
in my secret garden

Dragonfly Days

The California dragonflies are
as they should be – orange,
enormous, flying in formation
above green algae blooming
in the winter stream.

A hairy bug looks for a crevice
to hide his ugliness,
straight from the pages
of a horror book or a painting
by Hieronymus Bosch –
a creature that could have been,
but is not.

A blue heron floats down.
His majestic wings beat slowly
until he finds a reedy alcove
for an al fresco dinner. Transfixed,
I watch his shape-shifting ways –
a cruel flash of movement erupting
from a graceful silhouette
standing still as a priceless etching
amidst the rocks.

Once, I knew such dark-winged herons
watching us scare away the fish
from their river with our childish giggles.
Red-billed storks picked their lunch
of frogs and crickets from the trail
of freshly cut grass, its straight rows
measured by the motion
of my uncle's scythe
across the meadow.

Like long-legged pets,
storks followed the man
who fed them. They paid no notice
to a silent child trying to catch
a butterfly in her small hands,
watching bright blue dragonflies
over a ditch filled with rainwater
and forget-me-nots.

Blue and orange, the dragonflies
still haunt my memories, hovering
above the smooth surface
of long forgotten stream,
beneath the tranquil expanse
of high noon sky.

*

Sapphire

My tiger orchid blooms again
for the third time already

It looks at me shyly
with topaz eyes

thinking, I'd remember
that night, that music
of togetherness –

*Expand, expand, forever
expand* – our hearts fill

with Cosmic Light of
a thousand Suns –

liquid and flowing
to heal and purify

We thank, we praise
the One Love

that blossoms
in emerald gardens

in sapphire flames
and bright tiger eyes

NOTE: First published in *Rose Always - A Love Story* (rev. 2020).

Arbor Cosmica

for my children

No fear, no hate, not even a mild dislike* —
we leave our heavy burdens, shards of memories
broken, all too broken, at the bottom of crystal stairs
beneath clouds of white camellias, petals swirling
through air like the snow of forgetfulness

Perfect symmetry of blossoms
points the way — up, up, always up
rainbow crystal stairs, revealed
one by one as we ascend — inwards,
outwards — dancing spirals of our DNA

We get to know this place — these depths,
these heights — for once, for all lifetimes

With each step, pure notes resonate
and expand into clear, spacious chords —
the music of the spheres rings out, wave by wave
expanding from our open hearts

Each chord — harmonious, different —
each melody in this vast symphony
sweetly twines around another, and another
until all are One Song, One Wisdom —
of stem and flower, of leaf and root
in this Cosmic Tree of humanity

Arbor Cosmica —

We have been here
all along without knowing

NOTE: First published in the *California Quarterly* 44:1, 2018.

June in Gold and Blue

> *"It was June and the world smelled like roses. The sunshine was like powdered gold over the grassy hillside."*
> ~ Maud Hart Lovelace

Hidden among stiff, broad, dark-green leaves, straight from
an exotic isle, ripe bunches of loquat glow in rich sunrays
like "powdered gold" scattered on slopes across the valley.

I am content to share a loquat, juice dripping down
my chin, with a woodpecker that cut a groove in one side,
tasting its tart sweetness. With a shrill call, the bird flies
along a sine wave — rising, falling — too heavy for its wings.

I thought it was a parrot, one of our Pasadena invaders,
relentlessly chased away by my resident finches and doves.
I was relieved to see a bright, scarlet spot on its head,
black and white striped wings, peeking beneath the branches.

"Hello, my dear. Welcome to my June Paradise. Please enjoy
the fruit on the top. I cannot climb so high Let's share these
life-giving delights." The bird will not stay long. Its departure
will leave a gash of absence, stretching shadows in its wake.

Just like that dolphin, years ago, that joined our boat trip to
Catalina, jumping above waves with glee - we had to laugh.
The dolphin laughed too, teasing us with ephemeral dance,
contours outlined against the blue expanse of water and air.

Just like the striking, gold-furred grizzly bear, a mountain
of primeval power, curling to sleep on my lawn. Misiek.
My Protector. I'd swear I saw him once, at sunset. He came
to my Oasis to rest, dream lucid dreams about me —

as I eat luscious loquats straight off the tree, listen
to euphonious birdsong, gaze at the azure clarity
of endless sky. Serene, I am here, where I belong.
The taste of summer fruit. One June after another.

Imagine — A Poem of Light

> *... a cloud that scatters pearls*
> ~ Rumi

Are you an apple? Or perhaps
a ripe seed inside an apple of light?
You are snug and safe in the core of a torus
of light rays. You are wrapped in white
silk of light. Rays come from your crown into
toes, surrounding you with a bright cocoon,
of magnetic lines. Six winged angels stand
on all sides, watching over you.

No angels? Are you a fountain, then?
Your heart — the spring of goodness.
Liquid light overflows from within you.
Your heart-beat marks the smooth rhythm,
the gentle pulse of the sky of the sky of the sky.
The light! This miracle you forget about
every day as your blood carries your
heart-light into every cell of your body.

Not a fountain? A star, perchance?
Or, maybe, two stars. A large one brightly shines
on your chest, its rays straight and dazzling.
Multicolored sparkles dance in the brightness
of your aura. See, the second star blossoms
right above you, as radiant as the heart star?

Here you are: an arc between stars,
a lucid rainbow of ancient gold
still shining, shining, shining —

NOTE: First published in *Into Light. Poems and Incantations*, 2016.

DOROTHY SKILES
Seventh Poet Laureate of Sunland Tujunga
2012-2014

Dorothy Skiles says that poetry is in her DNA: "It's a way to interpret thoughts and emotions in an engaging way." She attended Biola College, graduated from Cal State Northridge in 1970, BA English. Served over 34 years with L.A. County, Department of Public Social Services, both in field work and administration. Since 2010, fellow founder and member of the Village Poets of Sunland-Tujunga (S-T) and served as S-T's Poet Laureate 2012-2014. Poems appear in the *Altadena Poetry Review Anthology 2016, 2017, 2018, 2019* (Pushcart Prize Nominee 2017). Poems also appear in *Meditation on Divine Names* 2012, *From Benicia With Love* 2013, *Altadena Poetry Review,* 2020, and in newspapers and online. She published four chapbooks (two in collaboration with fellow poets). "The Coyote's Howl" was a winner of the Monthly Poetry Contests of California State Poetry Society in March 2020. Skiles is also a Member of P.E.O., a philanthropic organization that promotes educational opportunities for women.

Taking the Old Road

Long before the 210 Freeway
was king -

I'd hug the old road taking
Foothill from Sunland
to Sylmar and back.
Sun, fog and wind
taught me well her ways
where the road narrows
where the road curves.
In the foothills
when the rain came
it came in a deluge.
Water cascading from
big rigs left me blindsided
like rainy days at work
drowning in deadlines
unaware of a looming crisis
real or manufactured
just around the bend.

NOTE: First published in *Altadena Poetry Review Anthology 2016*, Pasadena: Golden Foothills Press.

Yesterday's Roses

My arms are full of yesterday's
roses, once carefully placed in a
finely etched glass vase,
now dried and faded
from the sun's rays peeking
through the patio door
during these unseasonably
warm winter days.

Before the sun falls below our
beloved Verdugo Mountains,
I remove what remains from
the vase, recalling the pleasure
of such a gift from him who
loves to tend the garden
with hands and heart familiar
with the soil in all seasons -

These hands I love.

NOTE: First published in *Altadena Poetry Review Anthology 2017*,
Pushcart Prize Nomination 2017.

Winds

Early Autumn calls...

and Santa Ana winds whirl and bend
the half-barren white birch trees
before early dawn when
first day's light dances among
Sunland-Tujunga's old oaks.

Early Autumn calls...

Winds howl through the San Gabriels
until late afternoon brings calm,
and the promise of
the red hawk's tranquil flight
above the Wash before dusk falls.

Portland's Fog

Portland's foggy morning,
my raspberry coat buttoned
up to my throat, though
chilled, I smile as
childhood memories
play with my heart.

At church,
a burlwood urn holds
my sister's ashes,
encircled in a wreath
of red and white roses.
All meaningful conversation
 between us cease...

> *for she is speechless*
> *and so am I.*

I wonder what my dear sister, Barbara, who died in October 2019, would say about the corona virus? I know what she'd say, *"This will pass, everything will be alright."* Then she'd take her easel, canvass and paints and drive to a quiet field of flowers and create something beautiful! That's how I'll always remember her. *Happy Birthday, Barb...*

The Scourge of 2020

Alone, without a mask
I wander in my garden of
Peruvian lilies, lined-up
parallel and proud along
our newly painted fence.

Imagination takes hold, takes
me beyond the boundaries of
corona edicts where fields of
bright pink and yellow lilies
awaken in May's morning sun.

Surrounded by vibrant lilies
gathered in one place, I'm calm -
for they freely sway in the wind,
oblivious to the corona scourge.
    I sigh at such beauty unburdened.

The Coyote's Howl

*January's draught
portent of a scorching
summer to come…*

The San Gabriel Mountains
and Verdugo Woodland's
are but a tinder box-
terrain covered with
chaparral, a dry dense
stubborn thicket -
fuel for wildfires.
On summer nights beneath
the full moon's light, coyote's
coat the color of nickel.
Her features gaunt, gait less
confident, yet her sense
of smell remains keen.

From dusk to dawn
she traverses the ridges,
the low-lying hillsides
hunting rodents and rabbits.
She often treks into
neighborhoods, climbing
fences as swift as a thief.
The coyote is not too proud
 to forage for plums,
berries or pears.

This fall as the Santa Ana
winds rage, I'll listen
for the coyote's howl,
wondering if she'll
make it through
the threat of famine,
the peril of wildfires,
sure, to come!

Deep in My Dreams

In the middle of the forest
there is a house,
unafraid, I walk in.

Deep in my dreams

Weariness enfolds me
bringing me to my knees,
I lay by the cold, stone fireplace.

Deep in my dreams

God's Spirit is translucent.
I am transparent, for
Her Truth is very near.

Deep in my dreams

I awaken, unafraid,
to a house with
no windows, no doors.

ELSA SAMKOW-FRAUSTO
Eighth Poet Laureate of Sunland-Tujunga
2014-2017

ELSA SAMKOW-FRAUSTO. was born in Buenos Aires. The Foothills of Sunland-Tujunga have been her longest home after many years of wandering. She is happy with her 5 grandchildren who keep her tired and refreshed as only new life can. She has lived in Tujunga under the shade of oaks and with the nightly scent of chaparral and sage for over thirty years. She has been active in the local literary community as a member of the Chuparosa Writers, editor, and organizer of poetry readings. She hosted Camelback Readings to 2010 and Wide Open Readings from 2014 at the Sunland-Tujunga Library where she also showcases the Poem of the Month by local poets. Her poems in English and Spanish have appeared in many literary journals. She also publishes translations. From 2014-2017, Elsa was Poet Laureate of Sunland-Tujunga. In 2019, in collaboration with Alice Pero, she wrote a poetic dialog, *Sunland Park Poems* (Shabda Press, 2019).

Going

How many times this road, this river,
these mountains, the gorge opening like a mouth.
And we are going west, sun at our backs,
either pilgrims or explorers,
cutting the air with the speed
of breath and want.

How much is allowed in the space of a life,
how little remains,
how much was there at the beginning,
little we knew.

May be enough.

Late into the Night

do you feel my arm
circling your chest
like a gentle bear paw
would to find its home?

I like to think you do.
Then go on sleeping.
While I get up,
find this pencil, scrap of paper,
write.

Here, Alive & Awake

Four figs at 1 am.
And not until the fourth
did I look into the meaty
half between my fingers.
Kaleidoscope of purple flesh
or a dilated pupil
staring into my own.

Two hours away from
the ungodly time
and sleep doesn't come
instead these words.
I think they are the beating
of a heart, not my own.
The one night beats
while the earth turns
and the words echo–
I am here, I am alive.
I am here, I am alive.

I No Longer Question I'm a Poet

no longer question if I love You,
my Lord and my God.
Pursued by You from before
my eyes first opened
to the world, and my mouth
searched for food.

In my wandering, I gave You
a name made of loose syllables
like shiny pebbles.
Not Your name, just one
in my own likeness.

You, my Creator, who spelled me
in Your likeness.
In the sea of years, here I am.

In Your presence.

Long Math (for Ander)

He asked how long you and I had been together.
I said longer than apart.
Our childhoods could not have crossed paths-
you, in a country with a V for initial sound
and I, with an A and a river more yellow than silver.
Yet we met in M, a country like a palm with fingers
stretched into a fan.
And, all the rest, is the beating of our hearts and a
subterranean river and shared mountains and the
children of our children.
And, sometimes, the long math of our years together
gets the numbers wrong.

You surprise me.

I Offer You a Moratorium on Race

a meeting on the mountain top
of your choosing.
We'll take the longest road trip
with windows open and radio blasting.
I'll turn to you and you to me
and all we'll see are the blue/brown
fish of our eyes in a sea of air.

We'll learn each other's language
and speak it in the thickest of accents.
The words rolling in our mouths
like sugar coated sour gummy worms.

I'll say I love you with a smile.
You'll think I said I'm hungry.

And, I am.

PAMELA SHEA
Ninth Poet Laureate of Sunland-Tujunga
2017-2020

PAMELA SHEA, the 9th Poet-Laureate of Sunland-Tujunga, is a poet who chronicles her life through verse. Pam was raised in the foothills community of La Crescenta and studied at the University of Redlands. Her professional life has included medical office work and teaching in the fitness field. She has a long history of community service, which she has combined with her writing. She is a proud mother of three and grandmother of two. Pam finds inspiration in family and nature as well as in triumph and strife. As Poet Laureate, she has enjoyed "taking poetry to the people" at many venues around the community as well as participating in local 4th of July parades. Her work has been featured by Windsong Players Chamber Ensemble and choreographed by California Contemporary Ballet. She participated in the Gathering of California's Poets Laureate at McGroarty Arts Center, hosted by California State Poet Laureate Dana Gioia, as well as Lit Crawl L.A. and the NEA Big Read of the Los Angeles Public Library. Poetry has been her lifelong passion and therapy which she recently has combined with photography. Pam's work has been published in *the cherita*, and multiple editions of the *Altadena Poetry Review*, California State Poetry Society's *California Quarterly*, and *Spectrum* chapbooks.

Glowing Girl

Who is that girl
With the face all aglow?
From whence came her joy
And that vision of life?

She seems a stranger now
As she drifts through my memory;
I weep at the passing
Of this one I once knew.

Who do I see now
When I look in the mirror?
My mother, my sisters,
My daughters, or me?

"Who are you?" asks Caterpillar,
Who, who, who drumbeat in my brain;
A barn owl flies in the darkness,
Who, who, who is my mournful strain.

Who am I, my spirit queries,
Who, who, who echoes across years.
Answers seep into my bloodstream,
Who, who, who I ask through my tears.

Who is of no significance,
Who, who, who no longer matters;
Life is made up of such questions,
Who, who, who particles scatter.

NOTE: first published in *Altadena Poetry Review Anthology 2019*, edited by Teresa Mei Chuc and Hazel Clayton Harrison (Shabda Press).

Eulogy for Night

A new day approaches;
apprehension increases;
I must make the most
of the hours which come.

The dawn is ever nearer,
while time seems so fleeting;
I grow in wonderment
at great mysteries beyond.

The daylight is coming,
rising ever so swiftly;
and the seconds are humming
with the music of life.

What may come with this day,
I cannot face weakly;
be it joy, be it sorrow,
I shall greet it with love.

The future is not distant;
it is here; it is now;
every moment, each instant
is for all to enjoy.

So smile, my friends,
and walk with me bravely;
for time holds no end,
only unseen horizons.

Garden Visit

Memories surface,
Like lotus rising from depths.
I hear Mother speak
From majestic pagoda;
Her great-grandson hears.
Teardrops kiss koi in pond;
Unending circles ripple
Beyond time and space.

NOTE: first published in *Spectrum Special Edition, Poems for Mothers*
2019, edited by Don Kingfisher Campbell.

Lake Tahoe Vacations

Beneath mauve mountains
Clear blue lake waters flow,
The color of my father's eyes
And mine too.
Emotions rise from depths,
Rippling, spilling down cheeks.

Early morning risings
To water-ski on azure
Or transverse across snow;
I share memories with my son,
Whose eyes are blue too.
Cycles swirl like seasons.

NOTE: first published in *Spectrum Special Edition, Father Poems*
chapbook 2019, edited by Don Kingfisher Campbell.

Escondido

Hummingbird, rabbit, and crow,
Oh, earthbound creature spirits,
Take my message far beyond,
Where swirls the eternal song,
And ancestral spirits live.

In nooks and crannies hidden,
Existence between two worlds,
Mystery and happiness swirl,
Between earthly life and death,
And hidden treasure beckons.

Carry a message from me
To where I cannot yet see,
The ancestral spirit home.
Tell my loved ones they live on,
As I now sing Grandma's song,
In honor and thanksgiving,
So touch both dead and living.

Respecting what has long passed,
And truths that forever last,
Voices sing in wind's whisper.
Sky's expanse extends past sight,
Music hums all day and night,
On wing's flutter, out of sight,
Morning light comes in pink clouds.

Rosebuds and Lovers

The bud of a rose,
Layer on layer of petals,
Held tightly, perfectly,
Unfolding when the time has come,
Bursts open and a flower is born,
Releasing sweet perfume.

The heart of a lover,
Layer on layer of emotions,
Trembling, hidden, waiting,
When touched by the beloved,
Bursts open and a poem is born;
Sweet music fills the air.

Supermoon

Supermoon light spills into the room
And is tossed across my bed,
Alighting upon my head,
And awakening me to magic.

It beckons me to arise,
And I tiptoe through the house,
Trying to be as quiet as a mouse,
So as not to disturb the mood.

The backyard is illuminated,
Aglow in celestial light;
Hidden corners become bright,
As spirits are aroused and uplifted.

The air is startlingly quiet;
All earth seems to be caught in the spell;
Ah, Moon, what secrets we can tell,
As we commune this summer's eve.

Wash Wonderland

Alice falls
Through the looking glass
Surfacing
In the wash

In the distance a dog howls
In trees birds flutter
She whistles
To her friends

Overhead
A flock of geese fly, fly, fly
They call, sing
Reconfiguring

Hummingbird flits
From flower to flower
Mesmerizing
With the whir of wings

A crow caws, caws, caws
Seemingly scolding
In no hurry
To vacate its post

West to east
Sky pushes past moon
On its way
To golden sunrise

Indulge dear Alice
She is quite harmless
Carefully she steps

Sauntering along, sauntering along, sauntering along

In the past she ran
Trying to escape
Now she hops and skips
Into the future

When she leaves
It will be blessing
She will fly, fly, fly
Somewhere far beyond

Perhaps north
To mountains
Or south
To deserts
Maybe east
To sunrise
Or west
To ocean sunset
Won't you please join Alice
When you are able?
Wonderland exists
Wherever one chooses

NOTE: first published in *California Quarterly California State Poetry Society Volume 44, Number 1*, edited by Maja Trochimczyk.

ALICE PERO
Tenth Poet Laureate of Sunland-Tujunga
2020-2021

ALICE PERO's poetry has been published in many magazines including *Nimrod, National Poetry Review, River Oak Review, Poet Lore, The Alembic, North Dakota Quarterly, The Distillery, Fox Cry Review, The Griffin,* and *G.W. Review,* and anthologies *Coiled Serpent, Wide Awake, Altadena Poetry Review,* and others. Her book of poetry, *Thawed Stars,* was praised by Kenneth Koch as having "clarity and surprises." Pero is a teacher of poetry to young children in public and private schools since 1991. She is also the founder of Moonday, a reading series which has been on-going in the Los Angeles area since 2002. Ms. Pero has created dialogue poems with over 20 poets. Pero is an accomplished flutist who has created the performing group, Windsong Players Chamber Ensemble.

Old Oak of Sunland/Tujunga Library

>   on the Occasion of Laying the Tree to Rest,
>   January 13, 2020

Old oak, you have watched us long
while we trampled the underbrush
nearly 100 years

You watched
while we turned forest floors
into highways and sidewalks
finding comfort in books
inside cool walls of cement
and stone

Once you baffled the sun*
with your thick, fertile branches
your Old Women** friends
teaching us the prayers of the Tongva
though they, too, were almost gone
by the time your seed sprouted

We are grateful for your shade
your outstretched arms
as children ran about under you
shouting and playing
feeling spirit spreading grace

We are grateful for the grace
all live oaks give
more than just precious oxygen
something of an ancient time
when trees were sacred

Now we must send you back
to the earth from which you came
with hope that the spirit of trees
remains in your seed

NOTES:

* In 1910, a Los Angeles Times correspondent wrote about Sunland: *In the center of town the oaks are so thick that that the sun is baffled*

** "Tujunga" in the native Tongva language means "the old woman"

The Day of Nothing

When the day rolls out, a jelly-coated pancake
you sit in sweetness, sticking in sugar
feeling like you don't care about anything
you have a nothingness that is filling
a donut, empty calories that inspire poems

When you lie in a hammock,
swinging without care in summer sun,
the world, like a heavy stone, drops out from under
a symphony forms from one note
a parade of colors leaps into view
from one tiny paint drop

When the day holds no promise
laziness coming with slow drizzle of rain
windows fogged in
you swell and jump out while
lions chase wildebeests
dogs bark and bite their tails
warriors charge through burr-filled fields
worlds meet and collide
you burst and scatter into rollicking thunder
disappear without a trace of sweet or sour

Barter

I will trade a memory of oatmeal
(the one with the really sweet milk)
for a taste of potato chips, very crisp

The coffee on the airplane that
made me high I will give
for the belly laugh when George on Seinfeld
rescued the golf ball from the whale

But if you didn't save that one
I'll trade an old Ernie Kovacs Show
for a glimpse of the Degas dancer girl at the Met

I will exchange the feel of satin
on my first prom dress (bright blue)
for six orange peels dried in the
softest sun of summer

Will you take the smell of asphalt in
spring, steaming after rain
for six ripe plums waiting in
the basket on the porch?

I can give you the grandchild's shy smile
when I gave her a ballerina doll
but you must give me the sound of
oranges falling off the tree
with the slightest bit of wind added

There is a sprig of bougainvillea, very red
that jumps off the wall,
What will you give me for it?

NOTE: Published in *North American Review* and *Cairns*.

Green by Water on St. Patrick's Day, Sunland

Today all my stories turned green
when I took a walk in the wash
where rain had made cracked brown earth
sprout green and yellow and purple
Leprechauns were disguised as mischievous lizards
scuttling across my path
The snakes did not bother any
They had been sent away by a being with a crooked stick
The rushing stream at the foot of the hills
crashed noisily over the stones
making nothing of drought-disaster-sayers
who had been deposited in the ocean
at end of stream's run
All our hot dry fissures filled

Rumors

They say that soon
the sun will be swept
into the sea
The moon will visit me
and tell me
how to rescue the sun

but I know these are only rumors

The sea keeps secrets in violent waves
and leaves me wondering

The sun burns alone
in scorching silence

but only I live to dream

NOTE: First published in *Thawed Stars*, 1999.

Trochimczyk & DeCenzo, April 2010; Skiles & Hitt, July 2017.

Village Poets at Independence Day Parade, July 2015.

Village Poets after Gabriel Meyer's reading at Bolton Hall Museum, January 2019.

Passing of the Laurels from Elsa Frausto to Pamela Shea, April 2016; L to R: Elsa Frausto, Dorothy Skiles, Marlene Hitt, Joe DeCenzo, Pamela Shea, and Maja Trochimczyk, McGroarty Arts Center.

Village Poets with Margaret Saine, February 2017: Kath Abela and Rick Wilson seated in the first row, Bo Kim in a Korean national costume, and Dorothy Skiles, Mira Mataric, Joe DeCenzo, Marlene Hitt, Pamela Shea, and Maja Trochimczyk in the back.

The Passing of the Laurels Ceremony, April 2017, McGroarty Arts Center.

Alice Pero & Vincent Reyes, McGroarty Arts Center, 4/2017; Maja Trochimczyk Senator Anthony Portantino and Suzanne Lummis, October 2019.

Toti O'Brien featured in Feb. 2019. L to R: Shea, Wilson, O'Brien, Futa, Torregrossa. Back: Trochimczyk, DeCenzo, Hitt, Dutton, Larsen, Wilson, Dutton, Werner, Hawley.

BIOGRAPHIES OF FEATURED & GUEST POETS

LIDA ABRAMIAN. In her early years Lulu combined her drawings with one-sentence or one-word comments to communicate the profound; they were published in newspapers weekly. Her first book was published while she was still in high school. She is educated in New York, and her work has been published in newspapers and displayed in libraries and art galleries. She is the author of a poetry volume, *Start Where You Are*. Her writings are invitations to life, living from within who we are and seeing the magnificence and the truth of who we are.

MILLICENT BORGES ACCARDI, a Portuguese-American poet, is the author of three books: *Injuring Eternity* (World Nouveau), *Woman on a Shaky Bridge* (Finishing Line Press chapbook), and *Only More So* (Salmon Press, Ireland, 2012). The beautiful covers are reproductions of paintings by her husband, Charles Accardi (his website is: charlesaccardi.com) She has won fellowships from the National Endowment for the arts (NEA), the California Arts Council, Barbara Deming Foundation, Canto Mundo, and Formby at the Special Collections Library at Texas Tech (researching writer-activist Kay Boyle). Her work has also received three Pushcart Prize nominations. Accardi's poetry has appeared in over 50 publications, including *Nimrod, Tampa Review, New Letters and Wallace Stevens Journal* as well as in *Boomer Girls* (Iowa Press), *Chopin with Cherries* and *Grateful Conversations* (Moonrise Press) anthologies. Her theater/book reviews appear in *The Topanga Messenger*. Past artist residencies include Yaddo, Jentel, Vermont Studio, Fundación Valparaíso in Mojacar, Milkwood in Cesky Krumlov and Disquiet in Lisbon, Portugal. She received degrees in English and writing from CSUN Long Beach and holds a Masters in Professional Writing degree from USC.

SHARON ALEXANDER recently relocated to Benissa Costa, Spain overlooking the Mediterranean Sea. Her chapbook, *Instructions in My Absence*, won first place in the Palettes & Quills 5th Biennial Chapbook Contest and was released May 2017. *Voodoo Trombone*, Sharon's previous chapbook, was published by Finishing Line Press, 2014. Her poetry appears in several publications including *Barbaric Yawp; Caliban On-line; Idyllwild Life Magazine; Naugatuck River Review; Pearl; Pinyon; Redheaded Stepchild; Santa Ana River Review; Slipstream; Subprimal Poetry Art*; and *Tiger's Eye*. You can also find her work in the following anthologies: *Beyond the Lyric Moment* (Tebot Bach, 2014); *In the News* (The Poetry Box, Summer 2018); *Poeming Pigeons* (The Poetry Box, 2015); and *Spectrum: 140 SoCal Poets* (2015).

ELIÉCER ALMAGUER is a poet and author of fiction who was born in Holguín, Cuba and has been living in Santa Ana, California. For many years Almaguer worked to organize literary workshops for diverse public groups. He has published the books "Canción para despertar al forastero" [A Song to Waken the Stranger], "Si Dios voltease el rostro" [If God Turned His Head], "La flauta del solitario" [The Flute of the Lonely Man], and "Distorsiones del shamisen" [Distortions of the Shamisén]. He has received, among others, the national poetry prize Adelaida del Mármol, and the prize Puerta de Papel.

CHRISTOPHER ASKEW. I write poetry because my mother did. I write poetry because my daughter wanted me off the couch. I write poetry to explore the mixed blessings of relationships and retirement. I write poetry to explore, model, and teach – often myself. I write the poetry I write in response to challenges of form, challenges of sound, and to John Barr's challenge for the 21st century: poetry that is robust, resonant, and entertaining. Pushcart nominated (*Altadena Poetry Review*), I have one published book, *Hotchpotch: Sonnets, Idylls and Random Bemusements*. My poems have appeared in Spectrum and the Altadena Poetry Review. I currently serve as editor at Merano Writers Press in Pasadena.

BETH BAIRD writes: "Poetry is an integral part of all my endeavors. I am a songwriter, a story teller, a musician, and a singer. I love spoken word, music, and theater. I have written more than 30 songs and poems. My poems have been published in the US and abroad. I am honored to be published in Serbia and was invited to Belgrade to read at the International Writer's Meeting. I have read my poetry on local tv and throughout Europe. I currently reside in Altadena."

JUDY BARRAT began writing poetry, short fiction and creative non-fiction, as a young girl, in the hope of creating pictures with words as her grandfather did with paint on canvas and has been sharing her thoughts and words at various poetry and music venues around Los Angeles. Her work has been published in quarterly journals and anthologies, including the *Pelham Parkway Times, the San Gabriel Valley Quarterly, World Enough Writers, Quill & Parchment* and in the *Wild Women of Words Anthology, Altadena Literary Review* and *Spectrum* magazine, among others. In 2014 Judy began to fuse her writings with a musical background of jazz and blues, both instrumental and vocal, and in of 2015 performed the first of three sold out, lavishly praised, one woman shows at the Gardenia Club in Hollywood with musical accompaniment. She continues to perform at open readings and especially enjoys performing with musicians and singers, weaving their magic around her words.

CILE BORMAN. Music is the motivating force in Cile's life. She has traveled all throughout the USA cultivating her singing voice and perfecting her audience communication stills. Cile has appeared in Liberia, West Africa, and throughout Germany. She was the opening act in Japan for the Temptations. From Anchorage, Alaska to Jackson Hole, Wyoming, from Seattle, Washington to Hollywood, California, Cile has become a popular performer. She got her start singing with the jazz orchestra at Roosevelt University in Chicago Illinois. She has lived in Lake View Terrace, California, since 1982. She and her husband, writer and keyboard player, Mike Borman work together on their songwriting collaborations: Cile writes the texts and Mike writes the music. In the ancient tradition of singers who sang texts that they wrote themselves, Cile has become a poet-musician. She is also a community activist, having served on the local neighborhood council, as Vice President of Lake View Terrace Improvement Association, and active member of other local organizations. She serves on the "LVT Friends of The Library" committee, was Vice President of the Small Wilderness Area Preservation (SWAP) and is President of the Fourth of July Celebrations at Hansen Dam Committee. More information: CileTurnerBorman.com.

MADELEINE SWIFT BUTCHER writes poetry, fiction and true life stories with recipes. She has had her work published in the *West Marin Review*, *Grateful Conversations: A Poetry Anthology* and the *California Quarterly*.

ELENA KARINA BYRNE. Former 12-year Regional Director of the Poetry Society of America and Executive Director for the AVK Arts Foundation, Byrne is a visual artist, freelance editor and lecturer, the Literary Programs Director for The Ruskin Art Club, and annual Poetry Consultant and Moderator for *The Los Angeles Times* Festival of Books. She designs poetry programs for the Craft Contemporary museum and sits on the advisory board for What Books Press. She was a final judge for the Kate and Kingsley Tufts Poetry Awards until 2018, and until 2019, a Georgia Circuit visiting poet. Elena received the 2015 Distinguished Service Award from Beyond Baroque's Literary Arts Center. Since 1991 Elena has organized or funded programs for the MOCA, the University of Southern California's Doheny Memorial Library, the Getty Research Institute at the J. Paul Getty Center, UCLA's CAP/Center for the Art of Performance, Columbia University, The Shakespeare Center of Los Angeles, and more. Her non-fiction work has appeared in *Slope*, *Poetry International*, *The Journal*, *OmniVerse*, and *LARB*. A Pushcart Prize recipient, Elena's poetry publications include: *Best American Poetry 2005*, *Poetry*, *The Yale Review*, *The Paris Review*, *American Poetry Review*, *The Kenyon Review*, *Ploughshares*, *Colorado Review*, *The Academy of American Poets Poem-A-Day site*, *Black Renaissance Noire*, *Narrative*, *New American Writing*, *Dublin Poetry Review*, *Volt*, *Verse Daily*, *Wide Awake: Poets of Los Angeles and Beyond*, *Poetry Daily Anthology*, and more. Her books include: *If This Makes You Nervous* (Omnidawn 2021), *NO, DON'T* (What Books Press 2020), *Squander* (Omnidawn 2016), *MASQUE* (Tupelo Press 2008) *The Flammable Bird* (Zoo Press 2002).

DON KINGFISHER CAMPBELL, MFA in Creative Writing from Antioch University Los Angeles, has taught Writers Seminar at Occidental College Upward Bound for 35 years, been a coach and judge for Poetry Out Loud, a performing poet/teacher for Red Hen Press Youth Writing Workshops, L.A. Coordinator and Board Member of California Poets In The Schools, poetry editor of the *Angel City Review*, publisher of *Spectrum* magazine, and host of the Saturday Afternoon Poetry reading series in Pasadena, California. http://dkc1031.blogspot.com.

ROSS CANTON is a poet, playwright, filmmaker, novelist, and director. His work has been published widely in literary journals in the United States, England, and Australia. He graduated from UC Santa Cruz where he studied under such luminaries as George Hitchcock, editor of *Kayak*, Gregory Bateson, and Norman O. Brown, and received his MFA in Poetry and Non-Fiction from Vermont College of the Fine Arts. His books of poetry include *Involving Residence, No Thanks, Walking Water On Earth, The Art of Naming*, and *The Endurance: Journey To Worlds End*, a lyric novel. He is also the author of *You Don't Know Me*, a novel, *The Light Where Shadows End*, a memoir, and a number of plays and stage adaptations. He is the Founder and Artistic Director of Studio Theater West in Santa Monica, and the founder/originator of Movie/Poem, Inc. a multi-media platform for cross-genre poetic expression. He lives in the Los Padres Mountains where he, his long time companion, and his four dogs often spend meditative afternoons contemplating the serenity of trees.

GLORIANA CASEY. A small girl dreams of being——everything. Does she succeed?—Not quite ------- but if variety is the spice of life, it's been a grand success. Ice skater with the once upon a time Ice Follies, artist, creating animal creatures from paint and rock, teacher; US office of Education grant for Creative Dramatics; arts reviewer for Midwest TV and a copywriter too---occasional actress and SAG/AFTRA member——and of course, a rhymer poet, dedicated to the proposition that more can be learned and retained through RHYME, than form note taking. After all, before writing, there was rhyme, meter and song! Writing on and on and even sometimes still tutoring, and having a wonderful time!

JACKIE CHOU writes free verses, rhyming poems, and Japanese short form poetry. Her work has been published in *JOMP Dear Mr. President anthology, Lummox, Creative Talents Unleashed* anthologies, and others. She was nominated for a Best of the Net in 2017 by *Hidden Constellation*.

TERESA MEI CHUC is the author of several poetry books, including *Red Thread* (Fithian Press, 2012), *Keeper of the Winds* (Foothills Publishing, 2014), and *Invisible Light* (Many Voices Press, 2018). She was born in Saigon, Vietnam and immigrated to the U.S. under political asylum with her mother and brother shortly after the Vietnam War while her father remained in a Vietcong "reeducation" camp for nine years. Her poetry appears in journals such *as EarthSpeak Magazine, The Good Men Project, Hawai'i Pacific Review, Hypothetical Review, Kyoto Journal, The Prose-Poem Project, The National Poetry Review, Rattle, Verse Daily* and in anthologies such *as New Poets of the American West* (Many Voices Press, 2010), *With Our Eyes Wide Open: Poems of the New American Century* (West End Press, 2014), *and Mo' Joe* (Beatlick Press, 2014). Teresa's poetry is included in the anthology, *Inheriting the War: Poetry and Prose by Descendants of Vietnam Veterans and Refugees*. She edited two volumes of *Altadena Poetry Review*, served as Poet Laureate of Altadena, and published books of poetry, including *Keeper of the Winds* (Foothill Publishing, 2014). Teresa teaches literature and writing at a public high school in Los Angeles and is founder and editor-in-chief of Shabda Press.

JEANETTE CLOUGH's 2014 collection, *Flourish*, was a finalist in the Otis College of Art and Design and Eastern Washington University annual book competitions. She has edited and reviewed for journals and served as Artist in Residence for the National Parks. Recent poetry appears in the *Laurel Review* and *Colorado Review*.

BEVERLY M. COLLINS is the author of the books, *Quiet Observations: Diary thought, Whimsy and Rhyme* and *Mud in Magic*. Her poems have also appeared in *California Quarterly, Poetry Speaks! A year of Great Poems and Poets, The Hidden and the Divine Female Voices in Ireland, The Journal of Modern Poetry, Spectrum, The Altadena Poetry Review, Lummox, The Galway Review (Ireland), Verse of Silence (New Delhi), Peeking Cat Poetry Magazine (London), Scarlet Leaf Review (Canada), The Wild Word magazine (Berlin)* and many others. Winner of a 2019

Naji Naaman Literary Prize in Creativity (from Lebanon). Collins is also a prize winner for the California State Poetry Society who has been twice nominated for the Pushcart Prize, once for Independent Best American Poetry and "short listed" for the 2018 Pangolin Review Poetry Prize (Mauritius).

BRENDAN CONSTANTINE is a poet based in Los Angeles. His work has appeared in many of the nation's standards, including *Best American Poetry*, *Tin House*, *Ploughshares*, *Prairie Schooner*, and *Poem-a-Day*. His most recent collections are 'Dementia, My Darling' (2016) from Red Hen Press and 'Bouncy Bounce' (2018) a chapbook from Blue Horse Press. New work can be found (or is forthcoming) in *Poetry*, *Poetry Northwest*, and *Terminus*. He has received support and commissions from the Getty Museum, James Irvine Foundation, and the National Endowment for the Arts. A popular performer, Brendan has presented his work to audiences throughout the U.S. and Europe, also appearing on NPR's All Things Considered, TED ED, numerous podcasts, and YouTube. He currently teaches at the Windward School.

BILL CUSHING lived in various states, the Virgin Islands, and Puerto Rico before moving to California. Returning to college after serving in the Navy and working on commercial ships, he earned an MFA in writing from Vermont's Goddard College. He recently retired after having taught at East Los Angeles and Mt. San Antonio colleges. He's published in *Aethlon*, *Brownstone Review*, *Mayo Review*, *Newtown Literary*, *Spectrum* (as one of the "Top Ten Poets of L.A. in 2017), both volumes of the award-winning anthologies *Stories of Music*, and *West Trade Review*. His current project, "Notes and Letters," combines poetry with music and can be found on Facebook and YouTube. Bill's book of poems, *A Former Life*, was released by Finishing Line Press and is available from Amazon. He was named among the Top Ten L. A. Poets in 2017 as well as one of 2018's "ten poets to watch" by Spectrum Publishing of Los Angeles along with winning the 2019 San Fernando Valley Chapbook Competition with *Music Speaks*.

MARSHA DE LA O was born and raised in Southern California. Both sides of her family arrived in the Los Angeles area before William Mulholland built the aqueduct that brought in water from the eastern Sierras. Her latest book, *Antidote for Night*, won the 2015 Isabella Gardner Award and was published by BOA Editions. Her first book, *Black Hope*, was awarded the New Issues Press Poetry Prize.

PEGGY DOBREER won Downey Symphony Orchestra's, Poetry Matters 2016 Contest. She has one Pushcart Prize nomination from Cadence Collective, and two books with Moon Tide Press: *Drop & Dazzle and In the Lake of Your Bones*. Peggy is featured in the first Aeolian Harp Folio Series by Glass Lyre Press and has been published in *Cultural Weekly*, *The Rise Up Review*, *Pirene's Fountain*, *For the Love of Words*, *Mas Tequilla Press*, *Malpais Review*, and *LA Yoga Magazine* among others. Peggy is a longtime educator and former dancer, who taught with Red Hen Press for Writing in the Schools, and was a Program Director for AROHO2015, A Rom of Her Own Foundation. She has curated and promoted other poets at venues in LA for 15 years. www.peggydobreer.com.

LINDA DOVE holds a Ph.D. in Renaissance literature and teaches college writing. She is also an award-winning poet of four books: *In Defense of Objects* (2009), *O Dear Deer*, (2011), *This Too* (2017), and *Fearn* (2019), as well as the scholarly collection of essays, *Women, Writing, and the Reproduction of Culture in Tudor and Stuart Britain*. Poems have been nominated for a Pushcart Prize, the Robert H. Winner Award from the Poetry Society of America, Best of the Net, and Best Microfiction. She lives in the foothills east of Los Angeles, where she serves as the faculty editor of *MORIA* Literary Magazine at Woodbury University.

ALEXIS RHONE FANCHER is published in *Best American Poetry, Rattle, Hobart, Verse Daily, Plume, Cleaver, Diode, Poetry East, Nashville Review, Pedestal Magazine* and elsewhere. She's authored five poetry collections, most recently, *Junkie Wife (Moon Tide Press, 2018)*, and *The Dead Kid Poems (KYSO Flash Press, 2019)*. Her sixth collection, *EROTIC: New & Selected*, publishes in 2020 from New York Quarterly, and another full-length collection (in Italian) will be published in 2021 by Edizioni Ensemble, Italia. Her photographs are featured worldwide, including the covers of *Witness, Nerve Cowboy, Chiron Review, Heyday,* and *Pithead Chapel,* and a spread in *River Styx*. A multiple Pushcart Prize and Best of the Net nominee, Alexis is poetry editor of *Cultural Weekly*. www.alexisrhonefancher.com

MARY FITZPATRICK is a fourth-generation Angeleno who holds a BA from UC Santa Cruz and an MFA from UMass Amherst. Her poetry career is divided in two parts, separated by 17 years. In Part II, her poems have been finalists for the Joy Harjo Poetry Prize and the Slapering Hol Chapbook Award, featured in *Atlanta Review, Mississippi Review,* and *North American Review* as contest finalists, and have been published in journals including *Agenda* (UK), *The Dos Passos Review, Askew, The Georgetown Review, Miramar, The Paterson Review, Briar Cliff Review,* and on-line by Writers at Work (L.A.), *Hunger Mountain,* and *Terrain*. Her poems have appeared in eleven anthologies such as *Wide Awake: Poets of Los Angeles & Beyond* and *Cancer Poetry Project 2*. She has worked as a communications and change manager in a large corporation, and as a marketing and development director for a non-profit school.

MICHAEL C. FORD is a poet, playwright and recording artist. He has been publishing steadily, since 1970 and credited with over 28 volumes of print documents. He's been featured on approx. 65 spoken word tracks that include California Artists Radio Theatre productions plus 4 solo recordings. Since 1985. His debut vinyl *{Language Commando}* received a Grammy nomination in 1987 and his *Selected Poems of 1998* earned a Pulitzer nomination on the 1st ballot. His poetic narrative titled *Vietnam/Peace Casualties* published on-line for November 3rd Club was nominated for a 2006 Pushcart Prize. His first CD document was *Fire Escapes*; was a 1995 entry from New Alliance Records & Tapes. His 2010 document is titled *20TH Century Goodbye*, a production collaboration of Michael Campagna and Larry Thrasher, both of whom brought their Psychic TV chops to the project. Hen House Studios has been promoting and marketing his CD *Look Each Other in the Ears [2014]*. That document, in both vinyl and CD formats features a stellar band of musicians, not the least of which were surviving members of a 1960s theatre rock quartet, The Doors. His most recent volume of poetry published by Word Palace Press is *Women Under The Influence*, 2016. He is the author of 27 volumes of poetry, published regularly since 1970.

JOYCE FUTA has been writing poetry since she retired in 2001. Her book *Lit Windows: A Book of Haibun and Tanka Prose* was published in 2017. She lives happily in Altadena, a dramatic change from the city life of San Francisco, where she lived for 50 years. She has recently discovered a new creative passion: ceramics, the process of which in some ways is not that different from writing poetry - an openness to whatever might be unconsciously evolving, attention to detail, and patient revising and refining.

WILLIAM SCOTT GALASSO is the author of sixteen books of poetry including *Mixed Bag, (A Travelogue in Four Forms)*, 2018, and *Rough Cut: Thirty Years of Senryu*, 2019 available on Amazon. In 2017 he was co-editor/contributing poet of *Eclipse Moon*, the 20th Anniversary issue of SCHSG. His work has been published in more than 235 journals, anthologies and on-line publications in more than fifteen countries worldwide. In addition, he's participated in 300 readings and appeared on TV and radio programs in Washington, New York, New Mexico and California. His next book *Legacy* is due out later this year.

JERRY GARCIA is a poet, photographer and filmmaker from Los Angeles who is too old to have been named after The Grateful Dead guitar hero. He has been a producer and editor of television commercials, documentaries and motion picture previews. He is currently producing Poetry Films based on his and the poetry of others. In 2006, Jerry was chosen by the L.A. Poetry Festival to participate in Newer Poets XI Series as part of the L.A. Central Library's Aloud Series. In April 2015 he was winner of Terry Wolverton's *dis•articulationsreader Poem* series. His poetry has been seen in *Askew, Wide Awake: Poets of Los Angeles and Beyond, Chaparal, The Chiron Review, Palabra, Verdad Magazine, KCET's Departures: Poetry L.A. Style*, Tia Chucha's *Coiled Serpent Anthology* and his chapbook Hitchhiking with the Guilty. Jerry is a past-director of the Valley Contemporary Poets and former president of Beyond Baroque's Board of Trustees.

JOHN Z. GUZLOWSKI is the author of *Echoes of Tattered Tongues*, a book of poems about his parents' experiences in Nazi concentration camps; a portion of which was nominated for a Pulitzer Prize in Poetry. His stories and poems appear in such national journals as *Ontario Review, Chattahoochee Review, Atlanta Review, Nimrod, Crab Orchard Review*, and *Marge*, and in the anthology *Blood to Remember: American Poets on the Holocaust*. Garrison Keillor read Guzlowski's poem "What My Father Believed" on his program, The Writers' Almanac. Czeslaw Milosz said that Guzlowski's poems about his parents are "astonishing." Guzlowski is also the author of the Hank and Marvin mystery series and a columnist for the *Dziennik Zwiazkowy*, the oldest Polish daily newspaper in America.

CHARLES HARMON. Love to write, love to live, love to love, love to cook, love to eat. Teaching science is like cooking, cooking is like writing poetry, poetry is about life, love is about living, and living is about love. I love to write poetry. Long live love! Published story in local newspaper in fourth grade. Produced hundreds of poems (first love), songs, stories, articles, photographs, artwork, screenplays, novel.

Assembling collected poems, trying to get two books published. Won NSTA national science teaching award and $20,000 in 2001 for project, "Don't Be a Crash Test Dummy!" that teaches kids traffic safety, physics, chemistry, math. Use poetry, songs to motivate students, challenging them to write their own, codifying learning. Reviewed, edited, contributed to five textbooks for Houghton Mifflin. World traveler, five years overseas, 60 countries, lifesaver. Taught English, composition as well as sciences. Won SGVPQ poetry slam in Hollywood in 2006. Published in *Spectrum, Altadena Poetry Review, Ribbons, Haiku Windows, Haiku Society Anthology, Lummox, Prism Review, California Quarterly, Atlas Poetica*. Charles was named one of the "Top Ten Poets of the San Gabriel Valley" by Spectrum.

WILLIAM LLOYD HITT: A Californian, born in 1932, graduate of Verdugo Hills High School, 1949; graduate of University of Southern California School of Pharmacy with a Pharm D degree, president of the School of Pharmacy; U.S. Sargent and recipient of the Purple Heart (Korean War); pharmacist and manager of Hobers Pharmacy, Sunland, CA 1959-1995. For nine years he served as President of the Little Landers Historical Society that manages the Bolton Hall Museum in Tujunga. He is President Emeritus and charter member of the Tuna Camp Coalition formed to investigate, memorialize and make public the story of the WWII Japanese relocation camp in Tujunga in 1941-1943. Dr. Hitt received many awards and honors for his tireless and dedicated community service, including the titles of the Grand Marshall in Sunland Tujunga's Independence Day Parades. He belonged to poetry groups Chupa Rosa Writers and was a key member of the Village Poets, helping to organize monthly Village Poets Readings at the Bolton Hall Museum. His book of poems, *The Earth Time* was published in 2018 by Moonrise Press.

LOIS P. JONES was the shortlist prize winner for two poems in the 2018 Terrain Poetry Contest judged by Jane Hirshfield. Other awards include the Lascaux Poetry Prize, the Bristol Poetry Prize judged by Liz Berry and the Tiferet Poetry Prize, with work thrice listed for the Bridport Prize and the National Poetry Competition. Jones has work published or forthcoming in *Guerinca Editions* (2021), *New Voices: Contemporary Writers Confronting the Holocaust* (Vallentine Mitchell of London); *Narrative, Verse Daily* and *American Poetry Journal*. Her poem *Reflections on La Scapigliata* was one of 30 featured film-poem collaborations for the 2019 Visible Poetry Project. She is the Poetry Editor for *Kyoto Journal* and the host of Pacifica Radio's Poets Café on KPFK. Her first collection of poems *Night Ladder* is published by Glass Lyre Press.

GEORGIA JONES-DAVIS grew up in Northern New Mexico and Southern California. A former Los Angeles Herald Examiner editor, Los Angeles Times Assistant Book Editor and former free-lance journalist, Georgia's poetry has appeared in various publications including *West Wind, The California Quarterly, Brevities, The Bicycle Review, Nebo, Eclipse, poethicdiversity, Ascend Aspiration* and *South Bank Poetry*, London. She served as a board member of Valley Contemporary Poets for three years. Georgia was honored as one of the 2010 Newer Poets by the Los Angeles Poetry Festival and the Los Angeles Public Library ALOUD series. She is the author of two chapbooks, *Blue Poodle* (2011) and *Night School* (2015), by Finishing Line Press.

CE (CHRISTINE) JORDAN has performed and created unique dance/theatre work all her life. Her signature dance opus, *LA Breakdown*, a 6-part dance/theatre work, premiered in sections from 1984 to 1987 at Cal State LA, and came together at Fringe Festival LA in Fall 1987. She was bitten by the poetry bug in 1982 and has had her work published in *Armchair/Shotgun, Blue Satellite, Rivertalk* and other journals. Her true love, though, is blurring lines & meshing genres. She began staging her poetry and stories in 1996, performing with The Nannette Brodie Dance Theatre in 1996-97. Her signature theatre opus, *Notes on a Country Childhood*, full of touching stories and poems about her rural childhood in Ojai, CA, has been performed since 2009. Ms. Jordan's solo work includes *Map to the Stars* with Craig Kupka, pianist, which debuted at ArtShare LA in March 2016, and *Tinsel Town, Tall Tales of a Ballerina in Hollywood* (July 2017). *A Model Life*, her humorous run-down of life as a fashion model in the 70's and 80's, debuted in Dec. 2016. CE has her BA in dance/UCLA and MA in Theatre/CSULA. She has studied ballet and tap intensively, danced with The Moving Co. a Pasadena-based modern dance company, and worked with Bella Lewitsky and Miriam Nelson on stage and in television. Ms. Jordan spent 10 pretty marvelous years modeling on the runway, for TV, and editorial shoots, represented by Mary Webb Davis in LA and by Ellen Harth in NY. Her career teaching creative dance and theatre to children spans 25 years.

MANDY KAHN is the author of two poetry collections, *Glenn Gould's Chair* and *Math, Heaven, Time*. Her poetry is included in *The Best American Poetry* 2018 from Scribner/Simon & Schuster and was featured in former Poet Laureate Ted Kooser's newspaper column *American Life in Poetry*. She's given readings at Cambridge University, London Review Bookshop and Shoreditch House in England, at Motto in Berlin, at Colette in Paris, at Printed Matter in New York, at Davies Symphony Hall in San Francisco, and at many venues in Southern California, and has been interviewed by BBC Radio, Flaunt and The Los Angeles Review of Books. She frequently collaborates with composers to create new works that combine verse and classical music and was a librettist for Yuval Sharon's immersive opera *Hopscotch*.

MINA KIRBY is a retired mathematics professor. She has survived a broken washing machine, a broken back and a broken heart, all of which provide rich material for writing poetry and stories. She has for many years been a folk singer and sometimes songwriter. Plagued with health problems in recent years, her writing is part of coming back to life. Mina is the author of several books, including *Mathematical Dreams: Songs about Mathematics*, a cookbook, and eight chap books. Her poetry has been included in *Red Lights* (tanka), *The San Gabriel Valley Poetry Quarterly*, and *Poetry and Cookies*. She has presented her poetry at a number of venues, including Pasadena Art Talk. She lives in Altadena with her husband, daughter, two cats, a pet rat, and too many spiders.

MARIKO KITAKUBO is a tanka poet/tanka reading performer, born in Tokyo and living in Mitaka-city, Tokyo, Japan. She has published six books of tanka including three bilingual ones, *On This Same Star, Cicada Forest*, and *Indigo*. She has also produced a CD of her tanka entitled *Messages*. Mariko is an experienced performer who has presented her poetry at 234 poetry readings, events, and conferences, 177 of them overseas. She presented tanka in 51 cities in the world, in such countries as the U.S., Australia, Bulgaria, Canada, France, Germany, India, Portugal,

Tanzania, Switzerland, and the U.K. She hopes to encourage more poetry lovers worldwide to appreciate and practice tanka. www.en.kitakubo.com.

ANDREW KOLO (ANDRZEJ KOLODZIEJ) is a California artist, painter, poet and playwright born in Poland. He graduated from the Faculty of Fine Arts at the Nicolaus Copernicus University in Toruń with the title of Master of Arts in Painting and continued his studies in Paris and Los Angeles. He is the leader of the Krak Art Group that held many large exhibitions, for instance "Polish Identity" at the Bergamot Station in Santa Monica to celebrate Polish Regained Independence in 2018. Kolo's vocation is art, his passion is poetry. His poem: "America of an Immigrant" won the 1st prize in the national-wide poetry magazine competition: *Lucidity* Poetry Journal in Houston, Texas. Andrzej founded "Krak Poetry Group" in Los Angeles consisting of Polish-American poets and *9 ½ Poetry*, a group that promoted the work of young American poets. He is the author of a collection of poems and satirical arts *Polka Dot Tuxedo* published by Xlibris. Based on his script, *My Marilyn* was filmed. His play *The Trial of Dali* "was presented in Los Angeles, at the Hollywood Fringe Festival in June 2019, and in Sydney, Australia.

DEBORAH P KOLODJI is the California Regional Coordinator for the Haiku Society of America, the former moderator of the Southern California Haiku Study Group, which meets on the 3rd Saturday of every month at the Hill Avenue Library in Pasadena, and is on the board of directors for Haiku North America. Her first full-length book of haiku, *highway of sleeping towns*, was published recently by Shabda Press. (http://www.shabdapress.com/deborah-p-kolodji.html). With over 1000 published poems to her name, and four chapbooks of poetry, *Seaside Moon* (2005), *Red Planet Dust* (2006), *unfinished book* (2006), and *Symphony of the Universe* (2006), Kolodji finds inspiration in beaches, mountains, deserts, and urban life of Los Angeles County.

SHARMAGNE LELAND-ST. JOHN, 15-time Pushcart Prize nominee, is a Native American author, poet, concert performer, lyricist, artist and film maker. She is the Editor-in-Chief of the 18-year-old literary and cultural arts journal *Quill and Parchment.com*. She is widely anthologised and her poetry and short stories appear as well in many on-line literary journals. She has published five books of poetry. Sharmagne is editor of *Cradle Songs: An Anthology of Poems on Motherhood* (2012) winner of the 2013 International Book Award Honouring Excellence in Mainstream and Independent Publishing.

JAMES LEVIN has just completed his first book of poetry, *Where the Parrot Flies*. These poems are from 2003-2005. 2003 is the year he decided to focus on poetry, realizing he loved writing and reading poetry. He will begin his second book the summer of 2016. James is a graduate of the University of Wisconsin in Madison, spent his junior year abroad in Aix-en-Provence, France and after graduation, two years in French-speaking Cameroon, Africa as a Peace Corps Volunteer. James will begin his 31st year as a teacher for the Los Angeles Unified School District. He has three grown sons and is married to his lovely wife, Susan.

WAYNE ALLEN LEVINE is a writer, poet, philosopher, storyteller, impassioned public speaker and four-time author. LeVine's books include two collections of poetry: *Forgiveness for Forgotten Dreams* (2003) and *Myths & Artists* (2006). LeVine made his literary leap into the realm of nonfiction in (2012) with the release of his 3rd book – *Insights of an Ordinary Man* – published by Spirit Wind Books – a collection of essays and autobiographical vignettes, becoming his first Amazon.com international bestseller – which was followed by his 2nd nonfiction book *The Fourth Reflection*, published by Thomas Noble Books in 2016. Wayne Allen LeVine's poems and stories have been included in several award-winning journals and on-line magazines, such as *Rattle*, the Examiner.com, and several editions of the *Best-Selling Chicken Soup for the Soul* series, including *Chicken Soup for the Body and Soul*. A Midwestern son – born and raised in The Windy City, currently resides in Southern California with his wife and their two rock star sons.

STEPHEN LINSTEADT is a painter, poet, and writer. He is the co-author of *The Heart of Health; the Principles of Physical Health and Vitality*. His latest book is titled *Scalar Heart Connection*. His poetry is published *in Moments of the Soul* (Spirit First), *Solstice, Cradle Songs* (Quill & Parchment Press), Saint Julian Press, Poets on Site, and others. His paintings have appeared in *Reed Magazine, Badlands Literary Journal*, and *Birmingham Arts Journal* and can be seen at StephenLinsteadt.com. His most recent project is an anthology of poetry based on his paintings, *Woman in Metaphor*.

ELLINE LIPKIN is a Research Scholar with UCLA's Center for the Study of Women and teaches poetry workshops in Los Angeles. The author of *The Errant Thread* and *Girls' Studies*, she holds an MFA and a PhD in Creative Writing and has been in residence at Yaddo, Dorland Mountain Arts Colony, and the Virginia Center for Creative Arts. She has taught at Chapman University, Scripps College, and UC Berkeley. She served as Poet Laureate of Altadena from 2016-2018.

B. D. LOVE grew up in rural Michigan, where he attended a typical rural Midwest high school. Over the years, he earned his M.A. in English/Creative Writing from Syracuse University, he has quite serious writing altogether, formed several punk inspired bands from Syracuse to Dallas to LA and once more Syracuse. He returned to writing seriously after a freak accident shattered the elbow of his right arm, and he was told he'd never play guitar again. Since resuming writing, he has published in a great many journals and literally magazines across the nation, and has shepherded six books to print, four full length fiction books, one full length poetry book, and two chapbooks. His most precious new project is a song cycle for which he has written lyrics, with the gorgeous, soaring melodies provided by the great Maura Kennedy, another Syracuse expatriate. It's called *Villanelle: The Songs of Maura Kennedy and B.D. Love*.

SUZANNE LUMMIS' poems have appeared in *The Hudson Review, Antioch Review, Ploughshares, New Ohio Review, Plume, The American Journal of Poetry* and *The New Yorker*. Her most recent collection, *Open 24 Hours*, won the Blue Poetry Prize and was published by Lynx House Press in 2014. Previous full-length collections include *In Danger* (Roundhouse Press/Heyday Books) and *Idiosyncrasies* (Illuminati). Suzanne edited *Wide Awake: Poets of Los Angeles and Beyond* (Pacific Coast Poetry Series/Beyond Baroque Books), noted in *The Los Angeles Times* as one of The Ten Best Books of 2015. She is the recipient of Beyond

Baroque's fifth George Drury Smith Outstanding Achievement in Poetry Award. An influential teacher in Los Angeles, she leads private workshops and has taught for many years through the UCLA Extension Writers' program where she evolved courses in poetic craft, the persona poem, and the poem noir ("Poetry Goes to the Movies"). She is 2018/19 COLA fellow, an award from the Cultural Affairs Department to outstanding mid-career artists and poets. It comes with an endowment to create a new body of work. Lummis is the director of The Los Angeles Poetry Festival, which she founded with poet Sherman Pearl, and through which she produced nine citywide multi-literary events between 1989 and 2011. In the 70s, during CSU Fresno's now legendary era, Suzanne studied with Philip Levine, Peter Everwine and Charles Hanzlicek, and received an MA in English with a Creative Writing focus. Suzanne Lummis has at various times, on different occasions, been associated with the following schools and poetic sensibilities: the Fresno School, Stand-up Poetry, The Poem Noir, and Los Angeles Poetry.

RICK LUPERT has been involved in the Los Angeles poetry community since 1990. He served for two years as a co-director of the Valley Contemporary Poets. . He created the Poetry Super Highway (http://poetrysuperhighway.com) and hosted the Cobalt Cafe reading for almost 21 years. He's authored 25 collections of poetry, including "God Wrestler" and "The Tokyo-Van Nuys Express!", and edited "A Poet's Siddur", "A Poet's Haggadah", the Noir anthology "The Night Goes on All Night." and "Ekphrastia Gone Wild" under his imprint Ain't Got No Press. His poetry has appeared in numerous magazines and literary journals, including *The Los Angeles Times, Rattle, Chiron Review, Zuzu's Petals, Caffeine Magazine, Blue Satellite* and others. He edited *A Poet's Haggadah: Passover through the Eyes of Poets* anthology and is the author of thirteen books: *Sinzibuckwud!, We Put Things In Our Mouths, Paris: It's The Cheese, I Am My Own Orange County, Mowing Fargo, I'm a Jew. Are You?, Feeding Holy Cats, Stolen Mummies, I'd Like to Bake Your Goods, A Man With No Teeth Serves Us Breakfast* (Ain't Got No Press*), Lizard King of the Laundromat, Brendan Constantine is My Kind of Town* (Inevitable Press) and *Up Liberty's Skirt* (Cassowary Press). . He is regularly featured at venues throughout Southern California and works as a music teacher and graphic designer for anyone who would like to help pay his mortgage.

RADOMIR VOJTECH LUZA was born in Vienna, Austria to renowned Czech parents. The Tulane University and Jesuit High School Graduate (New Orleans) began writing and reciting poetry a year after graduating from college in 1986 He has served as Poet Laureate of North Hollywood, CA since 2012. A Pushcart Prize Nominee (2012), he is the author of 30 books (including 26 collections of poetry), and Writer's Digest and 2018 Highland Park Poetry Challenge Honorable Mention winner. Luza is the recipient of the 2016 Irwin Award (Book Publicists of Southern California) for "Most Creative Collection of Poetry" for his 400-page Magnum Opus, *Eros of Angels*. A freelance writer he has also recorded nine Spoken Word CDs. Luza, who speaks Czech and German in addition to English, had his poetry published in over 70 anthologies, literary journals, websites, newspapers, magazines, such as: *Askew, Boog City, Nerve Cowboy, Pegasus, Cultural Weekly, Journal of Modern Poetry, Bicycle Review, Poetry Super Highway, Covid-19 Anthology, Lummox, New Laurel Review, Spare Change, Los Angeles Daily News,*

Poetic Diversity, Altadena Poetry Review, An Eye For An Eye Makes The Whole World Blind, Men in the Company of Women, KYSO Flash, Boston Globe, Bucks County Courier-Times, Hudson Current, and *Spectrum*. The veteran stand-up comedian has featured his poetry over 100 times across the country in places such as St. Louis, MO, New Jersey, Philadelphia, PA, New Orleans, LA, Florida, New York, NY, Los Angeles, CA. Luza, is also a SAG/AFTRA/ AEA union actor, theatre, film and book critic and organizer/host/curator of over a dozen poetry reading series and open mics across the country, including *Unbuckled: No Ho Poetry*, now in its 11th year in North Hollywood, CA (co-hosted with Mary Anneeta Mann). atthetheatrewithRadomirLuza.com..

SHAHÉ MANKERIAN is the principal of St. Gregory Alfred and Marguerite Hovsepian School in Pasadena and the co-director of the Los Angeles Writing Project. As an educator, he has been honored with the Los Angeles Music Center's BRAVO Award, which recognizes teachers for innovation and excellence in arts education. His poems have won Honorable Mentions in 2011 Allen Ginsberg Poetry Award and *Arts & Letters Journal of Contemporary Culture*. Shahé was a Semi-Finalist for the Knightville Poetry Contest. He was the first place winner of 2012 "Black and White" anthology series from Outrider Press. Mankerian's *History of Forgetfulness* was a finalist at four prestigious competitions: the 2013 Crab Orchard Series in Poetry Open Competition, the 2103 Bibby First Book Competition, the Quercus Review Press, Fall Poetry Book Award, 2013, and the 2014 White Pine Press Poetry Prize. His poems have been published in numerous literary magazines.

MIRJANA N. RADOVANOV MATARIĆ, born in Novi Sad, Yugoslavia, earned her B.A, M.A, and Ph.D. in Linguistics and World Literature at the University of Belgrade, Serbia. Mira served as a librarian in the National Library of Serbia for 14 years followed by teaching at the University of Belgrade for another decade. In the USA since 1981, Mira taught college English, Creative Writing, Russian, English as a Second Language and Special Education, applying her expertise as art therapy. Mira co-founded and served as Present for "Women in the Arts" and edited the literary journal, *Collage* for nineteen years. Mira is known as a prominent free-lance writer, translator and translator-interpreter. She has published 46 books and a countless number of poems and stories in other publications. Mira has received numerous awards for her writing and creating cultural bridges at home and abroad.

GABRIEL MEYER. Poet-journalist Gabriel Meyer is an award-winning foreign correspondent who has lived and worked throughout the Middle East, the Balkans, and East Africa. He was especially acclaimed for his coverage of the first Palestinian intifada and of the Bosnian war. His reporter's diary on the civil war in Sudan, *War and Faith in Sudan* (Eerdmans), won ForeWord Magazine's Book of the Year award for essays in 2006. He has published poetry and two novels and is writing a long-term project, *The Testimony of Stones*, a "biography" of Jerusalem's Church of the Holy Sepulcher. His book-length poetry cycle, *A Map of Shadows*, was published by Tebot Bach Press in 2012. He is currently editing a collection of his Bosnian war poetry entitled *Dreaming of Wheat*. He lives in Los Angeles and is the executive director of the Ruskin Art Club (founded 1888), the city's oldest arts association.

MARIA ELENA MAHLER's poetry has been published in English and Spanish in *Badlands, Solstice, Quill & Parchment, Global Alchemy, Saint Julian Press* and Poets on Site. She was a finalist for the 2011 San Francisco-based Primer Concurso de Poesía Latinoamericana en Español, and is published in the anthology by *Colectivo Verso Activo*. Recently, her work was also selected for the Spanish anthology *Se Buscan Quijotes*, published by El Centro de Estudios Poéticos in Madrid, Spain. Maria Elena also co-authored the non-fiction book *The Heart of Health* (Truth Publishing Co.) and enjoys writing fiction. She was raised in the South of Chile. After graduating with a degree in Communications, she lived and worked in Mexico Canada, the Sonoran Desert of Southern California, and South America.

NAIA. In 1998, Naia discovered haiku through the works of Kobayashi Issa. She joined a small study group in Long Beach and has been writing haiku and other forms ever since. Naia's haiku were published in two prestigious anthologies in Japan: 1) *Masaoka Shiki Festival Anthology*, Ehime Prefecture Culture Foundation, Japan, 2001, and 2) *55th Basho Festival Haiku Anthology*, Basho Memorial Museum, Japan, 2001 (one of only 17 poets accepted from the United States). Her haiku, haiga, haibun, tanka, and other forms have been published in numerous books, anthologies, collections, e-journals, newsletters, and magazines in the U.S and internationally. Additional haiku-related activities include: co-editor, *bits of itself*, 2002 Haiku Society of America members' anthology; member, founding planning team for the first Haiku Pacific Rim Conference, 2002; editor, *above the tree line*, 2008 Southern California Haiku Study Group anthology; editor, *shell gathering*, 2009 Southern California Haiku Study Group anthology; judge, HPNC annual Haiku Contest, 2009; regional coordinator, Haiku Society of America 2009-2014; co-founder & moderator, Haiku San Diego, 2010 to present; reader, 23rdannual Two Autumns Reading, 2012; reader, Tea House Reading, Yuki Teikei Haiku Society Annual Reading, 2012; co-chair, Intervals, Haiku North America 2013 Conference; editor, what the wind can't touch, 2016 Southern California Haiku Study Group anthology. A video of her work may be found on Vimeo: *ants on the sidewalk*, a multimedia urban celebration by Naia, Deborah P Kolodji, and Gregory Longenecker: https://vimeo.com/60378349 Presented at Haiku Pacific Rim 2012, published in *Haiku Chronicles* in 2013.

TOTI O'BRIEN is the Italian Accordionist with the Irish last name. She was born in Rome, Italy, raised in Sicily and France. After touring Europe and Brazil with her itinerant theater, in the early nineties, she established herself in Los Angeles where she makes a living as a self-employed artist, performing musician and professional dancer. O'Brien's first book of stories, *Africa*, was published in 1990. It was followed by another short story collection, *Reversed Memories*, two illustrated children books and an essay collection, *Lanterna Magica*, gathering selected work out of her long-term collaboration with Italian journals and magazines. O'Brien started writing in English language in 2004. Since then, her poetry, fiction and non-fiction were published in hundreds of journals and anthologies in the US, UK, Ireland, Canada, India, Australia, and all over the world. Her most recent appearances include *ZiN Daily, the Harbor Review, Door Is A Jar, pethricor, CultureCult, Metafore, Gyroscope* and the *Mizmor Anthology*. Her work was nominated for Best of the Net, Best Small Fiction, Best American Essay, the

Pushcart, and various other prizes. Her memoir 'Nicotine' won a nonfiction prose award in 2018. Her essay 'Blur In The Front Line' won the Anthony Award in 2016. Besides her creative writing, she contributes articles and reviews about art, music, film, literature and civilization to several magazines. She also translates poetry and prose from the Italian, the Spanish, and the French. O'Brien's multimedia artwork was exhibited in group and solo shows in Europe and the US, since the early nineties. Her paintings, sculptures, collages and textiles were featured in many publications, and she has produced book covers and illustrations.

CECE PERI's poems have appeared in *Malpais Review, Luvina: Los Angeles Issue, Askew, NoirCon, Literary Alchemy, Beyond the Lyric Moment, Master Class: The Poetry Mystique, 1001 Nights, Spillway, Circus Noir, San Diego Poetry Annual, Wide Awake: Poets of Los Angeles and Beyond, Pratik: Los Angeles Issue,* and *MORIA*. She received the first Anne Silver Poetry Award and poetry awards from NoirCon, Arroyo Arts Collective, and honorable mention in the Steve Kowit Poetry Prize. A native New Yorker, Cece has lived in the Los Angeles area since 2003.

A.R. (ANDREW ROBERT) PETERSON. Born in Calcutta, India in 1942, AR Peterson is a British Citizen. In 1996, he became a naturalized American Citizen. He lives in Sunland, California. Beginning in 1960, Andrew was a technician in various government and commercial laboratories in England. He took MSc. and Ph.D. degrees in Medical Biochemistry at the University of Manchester, UK, and worked in Cancer Research at the Universities of Wisconsin and Southern California. In 1967 he was the co-author on a patent for the industrial production of gibberellin A7; this compound fools plants into producing fruit without being fertilized—so one gets seedless fruit. Peterson likes to think that he is partly responsible for the seedless grape. Imperial Chemical Industries, U.K., for whom he was working at the time, owns the patent. From 1986-2003, Andrew taught chemistry and science at LAUSD's Grant High School in Van Nuys, California. He has also worked for the EPA, NIH, The American Cancer Society, and NASA, producing over forty technical publications. He is co-inventor on two British patents. In 2003, Andrew took early retirement to write a textbook on chemistry, employing the historical approach that he had been using in high school. He is a published poet (sixty poems in two slim volumes), science fiction author, with books listed on his website ARPeterson.com. In 2017 he "completed" (it's actually up to the reader to complete) a non-fiction book entitled *Your Way*. In 2010 he published a science-fiction novel, The *Symbiote*, in 2011 a book of poetry, *Deconstructing the Rock*, in 2012, *Perestroika Poem*, and in 2018 his third SF novel, *Hubris*.

THELMA T. REYNA, Ph.D. has written six books: a short story collection, *The Heavens Weep for Us and Other Stories;* two poetry chapbooks—*Breath & Bone* and *Hearts in Common;* and three full-length poetry collections—*Rising, Falling, All of Us; Reading Tea Leaves After Trump*, which won six national book honors in 2018; and *Dearest Papa: A Memoir in Poems*, (Golden Foothills Press, 2020). Reyna's books have collectively won 14 national literary awards. As Poet Laureate in Altadena, 2014-2016, she edited the *Altadena Poetry Review Anthology* in 2015 and 2016. Thelma's fiction, poetry, and nonfiction have appeared in literary journals, anthologies, textbooks, blogs, and regional media, print and online, for over 25 years. She was a Pushcart Prize Nominee in Poetry in 2017; and winner of a California state legislators' award, "Women in Business/ Author, Most Inspirational" in 2011. Thelma is the founder and owner of an editing consultancy, The Writing Pros, based in Pasadena, CA, and of the multiple-award-winning indie book publisher, Golden Foothills Press. She received her Ph.D. from UCLA.

CINDY RINNE creates fiber art and writes in San Bernardino, CA. She was Poet in Residence for the Neutra Institute Gallery and Museum, Los Angeles, CA. She has created fiber art for over 30 years, exhibiting internationally. Cindy collaborates in Performance Poetry using her own costume creations based on her books. A Pushcart nominee. Cindy is the author of several books: *Knife Me Split Memories* (Cholla Needles Press), *Letters Under Rock* with Bory Thach, (Elyssar Press), *Moon of Many Petals* (Cholla Needles Press), and others. Her poetry appeared or is forthcoming in: *Anti-Heroin Chic, The Poetry Barn, Verse-Virutal,* several anthologies, and others. www.fiberverse.com

SHARON RIZK was born in Oregon during WWII. She has spent the majority of her life in various communities in Los Angeles County, although her first few formative years of schooling occurred in San Francisco. She received a BA in English Literature as a young adult, and returned to school as an older adult to earn an MS and a PsyD in Clinical Psychology. She recently retired as a Psychology Professor and has suspended her private clinical practice in CA while she pursues licensure based upon an interstate reciprocity agreement in New Mexico, where she built a mountain retreat near Santa Fe and now resides. She believes deeply in the healing power of the spoken work, mindful silence, and poetry. She is a published poet and has one CD collection of her original work, *The Shadow of Your Longing: Poems to Grow With* available on Amazon. Reach her at srizk@earthlink.net.

SUSAN ROGERS is a practitioner of Sukyo Mahikari—a spiritual practice promoting positivity. Her poetry is published in numerous anthologies and journals, including: *Altadena Poetry Review, California Quarterly, Carrying the Branch: Poets in Search of Peace, Kyoto Journal, Light on Light Magazine. Meditations on Divine Names: Anthology of Contemporary Poetry, Pirene's Fountain, Saint Julian's Press, San Diego Poetry Annual: The Best Poems of San Diego,* and *Tiferet.* You hear her read the poem "The Origin is One" in a short film on YouTube, at https://www.youtube.com/watch?v=rzPA9zeC0Qc. She was interviewed on KPFK by Lois P. Jones and nominated for a Pushcart Prize in 2013 and 2017. She is co-editor for the 2020 haiku anthology *A Sonic Boom of Stars*, and was one of the four international judges for the 8th Rabindranath Tagore Award. https://www.loispjones.com/susan-rogers.

ED ROSENTHAL. Poetbroker Ed Rosenthal's real estate poetry has been featured in the *Wall Street Journal, the LA Times and Urban Land*, the national magazine of the Urban Land Institute. He is known for performing poetry at Community Development Agencies, Los Angeles City Council investitures and gatherings of real estate developers. His nature/environmental poetry is found on Sierra Club sites and in California poetry journals. As a survivor of a desert ordeal, Rosenthal has been featured on *Fight to Survive* on The Outdoor Channel, and several Weather Channel presentations, LA Magazine, and *"The Story"* on National Public Radio. A volume of poems was inspired by this experience, *The Desert Hat* (Moonrise,2015).

MARY KAY RUMMEL is the first Poet Laureate of Ventura County, CA. Her seventh book of poetry, The Lifeline Trembles, has been published by Blue Light Press of San Francisco as a winner of the 2014 Blue Light Poetry Prize. Recent publications include poems in *Nimrod, Pirene's Fountain, Askew* and in the anthologies, *Woman in Metaphor* by Stephen Linsteadt; *Meditations on Divine Names* (Moonrise Press); *A Bird Black As The Sun* (Green Poet Press); and *Creativity and Constraint* (Wising Up Press).Mary Kay has received four Pushcart nominations, was 2013 winner of the Irish American Crossroads Contest in San Francisco. She teaches part time at California State University, Channel Islands and lives in Ventura. More information: marykayrummel.com.

SONYA SABANAC (née Zivic) was born and raised in Former Yugoslavia, a country that no longer exists. Disappeared like Atlántida and left its former citizens to carry a heavy burden of constant search for a home. Sonya was born in the City of Sarajevo, where she graduated from Sarajevo University School of Law. In the midst of the war that made her country gone, in 1992, Sonya left the county with her family and spent two years in Denmark living as a refugee. She immigrated into USA in 1994, and landed at Los Angeles, where she still lives. She was a passionate reader all her life and an ardent poetry lover, but she only started writing in her late forties. Sonya is a member of Los Angeles Westside Women Writers Group. Her poems appeared in *San Gabriel Valley Poetry Quarterly, Magnapoets, Poetic Diversity* and the anthology *Immigrant Women Shifting Balance Sheets*. Her book of memoirs is entitled *How I Decided to Go a Little Crazy*. In addition to writing, Sonya is also a photographer, working on a book linking short stories with images.

MARGARET SAINE lives in Los Angeles. After a doctorate in French from Yale, she taught Spanish at universities in California and Arizona. She writes poetry, haiku, and short stories in five languages and also translates other poets. Her books are *Bodyscapes, Words of Art*, and five haiku chapbooks. Poetry manuscripts ready for publication are *The Five Senses, Reading Your Lips, Words of Winter*, and *While Alive*. *Paesaggi che respirano* [Breathing Landscapes] of her poetry in Italian has been published in Italy. She has recently completed *As You Were Saying*, a dialogue with American poet William Carlos Williams. Saine's books of poetry *Lit Angels* (2017) and *Gardens of the Earth: According to Nature* (2019) were published by Moonrise Press. She is the Board Secretary of California State Poetry Society and Editor of the California Quarterly, where she publishes translation from Italian, German, Spanish, and French poets.

PARAM SHARMA is from Guyana (previously British Guiana) in South America. He is retired and has been living in Los Angeles for the past 40 years. He first came to the United States in 1968 for one unforgettable summer in New York City. He made his living primarily as a technical writer / systems analyst, having held positions in teaching (college, high school, and trade school), accounting, records management, tax preparation, real estate sales, mortgage financing, and commercial appraisal. Apart from reading and writing, his other interests are music, woodworking, PC tinkering and photography. Recently he established Carib House and began a book publishing avocation. He has one title in this endeavor and another one in process. The poem featured here is taken from his book of poems "The New Caribbean Man," which was considered for the Commonwealth Poetry Prize (U.K.)

in 1980. Param has a master's degree in English: Creative Writing from San Francisco State University.

SHAYMAA has been writing since she was a kiddo scribbling in a glitter gel-front lock diary. She has been an editor for Rind Literary Magazine since it´s inception. She has been published in *The Chiron Review, The Cal Literary Arts Magazine, East Jasmine Review, ISM Magazine* and the *Field Guide: Nature Poems*, among others. A previous Poet Laureate of the US read her work and told her it was excellent, which she is still immensely proud of. She has won various writing scholarships and contests, which also help to reassure her that her passion is something people might also enjoy engaging with. She hopes to embrace all her witchiest dreams by eventually owning a tiny house squirrelled away in a forest somewhere, and drinking tea and gardening to her heart´s content amongst many cats, horses and one Newfoundland. For now, she is living in the Netherlands while she works on her Master´s thesis about the Post-colonial potential of magic in current and Ancient Egypt.

RICK SMITH is a poet, blues harmonica player and clinical psychologist practicing in Rancho Cucamonga, California. Born in New York City and raised in New York, Paris and Bucks County, Pennsylvania by two accomplished artists. His father William A. Smith was a painter, photographer and illustrator for the *Saturday Evening Post, Mc Calls* and *Reader's Digest Condensed Books*. He did U.S. postage stamps and books with Edgar Rice Burroughs, Pearl S. Buck, book and record covers for Carl Sandburg. His portrait of Sandburg hangs in the National Portrait Gallery in Washington D.C. "St. Germaine District" is about him. Read more about the Sandburg connection in *Under The Sun* online 2019 or on Rick's web site (docricksmith.com). Rick's latest book is *Whispering In A Mad Dog's Ear* (Lummox Press, 2014). He also published *Hard Landing* (2010) and *The Wren Notebook* (2000) with Lummox. *Exhibition Game* (1973) is from G. Sack Press. As a musician, he can be heard on the soundtrack of Academy Award winner *Days of Heaven* and on recordings with The Mescal Sheiks, The City Lights, Music Formula, The Hangan Brothers and The Rick Smith Band...

KATHI STAFFORD. Born and raised in Texas, Stafford has lived in India and contrasting the memories of her childhood with the exotic impressions from her Indian sojourn is a frequent theme in her poetry. She is a member of the Westside Women Writers group, co-editors of *Grateful Conversations* anthology (Moonrise Press, 2018), and a contributor to the Portuguese-American Journal. She has previously acted as poetry editor and senior editor for *Southern California Review*. Her poetry, interviews, and book reviews have appeared in literary journals such as *Rattle, Chiron Review, Nerve Cowboy, Connecticut River Review, Southern California Review,* and *Hiram Poetry Review*. Her poetry has been anthologized in *Chopin and Cherries*, as well as *Sea of Change: Poems for Hitchcock*. She edited a chapbook about Beatrice for Galerie De Difformite, called *Beatrice Emerges*, and including poems by Millicent Borges Accardi, Susan Rogers, Maja Trochimczyk, and Jennifer Smith, 2011.

JULIA STEIN's seventh book of poetry *What Were They Like?* was published March 2013. In the last two years she edited two books of poetry: *Every Day is an*

Act of Resistance: Selected Poems of Carol Tarlen by the brilliant S.F. poet Carol Tarlen who died in 2004 and *Walking Through a River of Fire: 100 Years of Triangle Fire Poetry*. Stein is the 2011 Joe Hill Poetry Award winner. She has worked on an oral history project interviewing pioneers of the San Fernando Valley including children who grew up in Sunland-Tujunga in 1900-1920.

MELISSA STUDDARD is the author of a poetry collection *I Ate the Cosmos for Breakfast* and the young adult novel *Six Weeks to Yehidah*. Her short writings have appeared in a wide variety of journals, magazines, blogs, and anthologies, such as *The New York Times, Poetry, Psychology Today, The Guardian, New Ohio Review, Harvard Review, Bettering American Poetry,* and *Poets & Writers*. A short film of the title poem from *I Ate the Cosmos for Breakfast* (by Dan Sickles of Moxie Pictures for Motionpoems) was an official selection for the Trinidad and Tobago Film Festival and the Minneapolis St. Paul International Film Festival, as well as winner of the REEL Poetry Festival Audience Choice Award. Other poems have been made into car magnets, elepoem booth recordings, and Houston City Banners.

KONRAD TADEMAR WILK is an American poet living in Los Angeles. His works range from single sonnets to epic poems on themes including current events, myth, and philosophy. In addition to American subjects, his work is strongly informed by international events and history, especially those of freedom and oppression. Tademar's early childhood was spent in Poland where he was particularly influenced by the rise of the anti-communist Solidarity labor union. Following his return to the U.S., he studied philosophy and literature at Los Angeles City College where he was president of the Poet's Platform. He then went on to graduate from UCLA. He has appeared in Los Angeles venues such as the Onyx, Ground's Zero, Magicopolis Theater, Wilshire Art Gallery, and Pig and Whistle. In 1991, he founded the Witching Hour Poetry Gathering which has met continuously for over 20 years. Additionally, he is a founding member of the Pecan Pie Organization, dedicated to artistic promotion, stage performances. His poetry book *Fifty Sonnets, titles like labels only get in the way...* is available for purchase on line. Some of his stories and poems are available on the internet.

AMBIKA TALWAR is an India-born author, wellness consultant, artist, and educator whose vision is to realize her sacred destiny. Publications include: *California Quarterly; Collateral Damage; Grateful Conversations; Kyoto Journal; Chopin with Cherries; On Divine Names; St. Julian Press; Tower Journal; Tebot Bach; VIA-Vision in Action;* in Poets on Site collections; *Life and Legends; Enchanting Verses; Aatish 2* (Great India Poetry Contest); *The World Literature Blog; Quill & Parchment; Pratik* (2020) and others. She authored *4 Stars & 25 Roses* (poems for her father) and *My Greece: Mirrors & Metamorphoses*, a poetic-spiritual travelogue that explores our human purpose in a roving personal and mythical narrative. She currently serves on the board of California State Poetry Society. She offers intuitive wellness workshops and notes that poetry and healing go well together for language is deeply coded in our cells. An English professor at Cypress College, she lives in Los Angeles, and New Delhi, India. Look for her work on websites patreon.com/goldenmatrixvisions and creativeinfinities.com.

JUDITH TERZI is the author of *Museum of Rearranged Objects* (Kelsay Books, 2018) as well as of five chapbooks including *If You Spot Your Brother Floating*

By, *Casbah* (Kattywompus), and *Ghazal for a Chamber-maid* (Finishing Line). Her poetry appears in a wide array of literary journals and anthologies and has been nominated for a Pushcart and Best of the Net and Web. "Ode to Malala Yousafzai" was read on Radio 3 of the BBC and included in a study guide for the artist-in-residence program for State Theater New Jersey. She holds an M.A. in French Literature and taught high school French at Polytechnic School in Pasadena for many years, as well as English at California State University, Los Angeles, and in Algiers, Algeria. Visit her website @ sharingtabouli.com.

BORY THACH was born in a refugee camp located on the border between Thailand and Cambodia. His family immigrated to the United States when he was four years old. He served in the U.S. Army and deployed to Iraq in support of Operation Iraqi Freedom. He has an MFA from California State University San Bernardino. Fiction and creative nonfiction fall under the art of storytelling, while poetry for him is more of a study of language, an art form in itself. His work appeared or is forthcoming in: *Pacific Review, Urban Ivy, Arteidolia, Sand Canyon Review* and *Here We Are: Village Poets Anthology*. He recently completed a book of poetry dialogues with Cindy Rinne, *Letters under Rock* (2019) that has been presented as a quasi-theatrical performance in art galleries and museums in Southern California.

G. MURRAY THOMAS has been active in the SoCal poetry scene for over 20 years. He has performed throughout the L.A. area and beyond. He was the editor and publisher of *Next... Magazine*, a poetry calendar/newsmagazine for Southern California. *Next... Magazine* was published monthly between 1994 and 1998. *News Clips & Ego Trips*, a collection of articles from Next..., was just published by Write Bloody Press. His most recent book of poetry is *My Kidney Just Arrived*, published by Tebot Bach in 2011. His previous books are *Cows on the Freeway* and *Paper Shredders*, an anthology of surf writing. Thomas has also published five chapbooks, and has been widely published in various literary magazines. More information can be found at http://gmurraythomas.com/.

MARY TORREGROSSA's poems appear in *Bearing The Mask: Southwestern Persona Poems, Wide Awake: Poets of Los Angeles and Beyond, Voices From Leimert Park Redux*, poets of the World Stage in Los Angeles. Her chapbook, *My Zocalo Heart*, a collection of portrait and persona poems was published by the Finishing Line Press. Mary explains, "I am a story-listener. It comes as part of my job as an Adult School ESL teacher in the Los Angeles area. I have to "listen twice" - as the Quakers say. So in my subsequent story-telling I have created a gallery of portrait poems along with a tapestry of longer narrative poems." Mary's poems are rich in detail like gems kept in a music box.

YUN WANG is the author of two poetry books ("The Book of Totality", Salmon Poetry Press, 2015; and "The Book of Jade", Winner of the 15th Nicholas Roerich Poetry Prize, Story Line Press, 2002), two poetry chapbooks ("Horse by the Mountain Stream", Word Palace Press, 2016; "The Carp", Bull Thistle Press, 1994), and a book of poetry translations ("Dreaming of Fallen Blossoms: Tune Poems of Su Dong-Po", White Pine Press, 2019). Wang's poems have been published in numerous literary journals, including *The Kenyon Review, Prairie Schooner, Cimarron Review, Salamander Magazine, Green Mountains Review*, and *International Quarterly*. Her translations of classical Chinese poetry have been published in *The Kenyon Review Online, Salamander Magazine, Poetry Canada Review, Willow Springs, Kyoto Journal, Connotation Press*, and elsewhere. Wang was born in China, and came to the U.S. for graduate school in 1985. She is an astrophysicist at California Institute of Technology.

MARI WERNER'S work has been published in *Rattle, Altadena Poetry Review, Colorado Boulevard,* and elsewhere. She is the founder and co-host of the Open Words monthly poetry reading in Claremont, California, and is a frequent reader at poetry venues in the greater Los Angeles area. She is also the author of the *Workable Economics* website. She is retired from a career in technical writing and currently lives in Claremont, California in the company of an abundance of wise trees, wild birds, and a wealth of other life forms (including amicable human neighbors).

KATH ABELA WILSON created and directs Poets on Site, Tanka Poets on Site, and Caltech Red Door Poets. She holds salons and weekly tanka meetings with her husband Rick Wilson at their home, hosts tanka performance festivals in and around Pasadena, California, and welcomes visiting poets. Kathabela performs with Rick's accompaniment on flutes of the world in museums, galleries, libraries, and the local Storrier Stearns Japanese Garden. She has created more than thirty programs and themed anthologies containing international poets' work. She leads the online Facebook group Tanka Poets on Site, for several years giving daily prompts for tanka writing exercises. Tanka Poets on Site was presented on the Queen Mary at the Tanka Society of America's Tanka Sunday in 2013. She currently writes "Mapping the Artist," a weekly interview series with poets and artists, and hosts a weekly "Poetry Corner" for ColoradoBlvd.net, where she presents many tanka poets. Kathabela (her pen name is Kath Abela Wilson) uses her patient, beautiful 94-year-old mother's Maltese maiden name (Abela) as a centerpiece and inspiration. Kathabela and Rick travel the world together to math conferences (the summer of 2014 marked their fifth trip to China and Japan). She loves her work as TSA secretary, especially because it gives her close personal contact and friendship with members, and inspiration to collaborate with them even more closely.

MARIANO ZARO is the author of six books of poetry, most recently *Decoding Sparrows* (What Books Press, Los Angeles, CA) and *Padre Tierra* (Olifante, Zaragoza, Spain). His poems have been published in anthologies and literary journals in USA, Mexico and Spain. His translations into Spanish include *Poemas de las Misiones de California* by Philomene Long, *Buda en llamas* by Tony Barnstone and *Cómo escribir una canción de amor* by Sholeh Wolpé. He is the winner of the 2004 Roanoke Review Short Fiction Prize and the 2018 Martha's Vineyard Institute of Creative Writing Short Fiction Prize. Since 2010, he has been hosting a series of video-interviews with prominent American poets as part of the literary project Poetry.LA. (More information here: www.Poetry.LA). He is a professor of Spanish at Rio Hondo Community College (Whittier, California). Website: www.marianozaro.com.

www.ingramcontent.com/pod-product-compliance
Lightning Source LLC
Chambersburg PA
CBHW071659160426
43195CB00012B/1518